THIS IS A GIFT FROM:

AND THIS IS GIVEN WITH LOVE TO:

WOMEN GONE WILD

"Teach her about how money really works, and she can change the world."

- Linda Davis Taylor

"Money is only a tool. It will take you wherever you wish, but it will not replace you as the driver."

- Ayn Rand

"Never work just for money or for power. They won't help save your soul or help you sleep at night."

- Marian Wright Edelman

"Being rich is having money; being wealthy is having time."

- Margaret Bonnano

"The most valuable real estate in the universe is inside your soul."

- Matshona Dhliwayo

"For women, financial independence is a matter of necessity."

- Carrie Schwab-Pomerantz

"Some people think they are worth a lot of money just because they have it."

- Fannie Hurst

PRAISE

"We need more books like this that celebrate the success of women. Thank you."

- Top Talent Magazine

"Women Gone Wild is not only an amazing book it's a sisterhood of likeminded women who want to work together and grow! I recommend this book to any woman on any level of business."

- Heather Marianna, *Founder of Beauty Kitchen*

"There are so many women breaking through glass ceilings right now and I love that this book teaches us how to do that without fear!"

- Santia Deck, *Founder of Tronus Footwear*

"This book is powerful and a great example for women leaders of today."

- Sandra Bledsoe, *Revenge MD CEO*

PRAISE

"This is a diverse group of women who are wildly successful with wildly great stories worth reading."

- Los Angeles Tribune

"I absolutely love what Women Gone Wild represents! This is the time for women to shine and tap into our power and I love that this new book is helping guide the way to do that!"

- Jamie Anderson
2x Olympic Gold Medalist in Snowboarding

"Women Gone Wild is an invitation for women everywhere to rise. It is an inspiring rally cry to find the unstoppable, inextinguishable, powerful force that exists within all of us and to invite that part of us to step forward and lead."

- Rebecca Campbell
Bestselling author of Rise Sister, Rise

COPYRIGHT

TOP TALENT PUBLISHING
SELF IMPROVEMENT, BUSINESS DEVELOPMENT BOOKS

WOMEN GONE

WILD

THE FEMININE GUIDE
TO FEARLESS LIVING

• THE WEALTH EDITION •

RHONDA SWAN • HANALEI SWAN • DIANA VON WELANETZ WENTWORTH • DANA KAY

ISABEL FAGAN • STEFANIE BRUNS • CAMBERLY GILMARTIN • KAREN WHELAN

KORTNEY MURRAY • SHAR MOORE • TARRYN REEVES • BLAIR KAPLAN VENABLES

ADRIANA MONIQUE ALVAREZ • EBONY SWANK • BARBIE LAYTON • APRIL RYAN • MICHALE GABRIEL

ANIA HALAMA • MICHELLE BELTRAN • GENEVIEVE SEARLE • DANELLE DELGADO • ROBIN MULLIN

UBA

Unstoppable Branding Agency

We Turn Best Kept Secrets Into World Renowned Brands

WWW.UNSTOPPABLEBRANDINGAGENCY.COM

TABLE OF CONTENTS

"*The new way of successful entrepreneurship and business is through authentic, powerful collaborations. When we link hearts, intentions and dreams, we forge a web that will reach farther and impact greater than a net cast alone. As wild women, we have an opportunity to share our dreams and unite for the greater good of all.*"

- Danette May, Speaker, Author, and VIP Coach

"I'm excited to see more women stepping into their power as investors & entrepreneurs. This book will help open the doors for more women to believe they can do it, too."

- Kevin Harrington, The Original Shark from *Shark Tank*

DEDICATION

To our mothers, daughters, and sisters...to our girlfriends that are more than family...to all the women in our lives...we hug you, appreciate you and love you.

SPECIAL THANKS

To the mentors we've had, the trainers we've invested time and resources with, the bestselling authors we've learned from, the speakers we've been inspired by, and our individual teams that have supported us, we say thank you!

LETTER FROM THE EDITOR

BY JESSICA SHEEHAN

"If they ask you how rich you are, tell them to look inside your heart."

- MATSHONA DHLIWAYO

Dear Wild Writers and Readers,

The amount of wisdom around wealth shared in this book is both touching and abundant. Indeed, whether it is the traditional wealth of dollars and cents, or the more esoteric and intangible perspective of abundance, this book covers it all.

You are cherished and loved, and with great respect for your willingness to share from your hearts, the editing to this book has been minimal. May all readers experience your intentions, hear your voices, and learn from your stories. This book brings forth all the triumphs from tragedy, healing from hurt, and tenacious perseverance to unimaginable wealth. Therefore, the delivery of information may be in an atypical, less structured, and more free-flowing way.

You are uncensored. I would wish nothing less for such a fierce collaboration of women.

Readers should read this book now, and then read it again; continue to read it as you grow throughout your life. You will want to refer to its many lessons and nuggets often. For as you change, so will your impressions and understanding of this material.

You will find yourself giving this as a gift many times over. The messages contained within this manuscript offer such priceless and magical insight, that you will want every woman in your tribe to know of its secrets.

It's precious, magnificently crafted, and invaluable – just like you.

-Jessica Sheehan,
Top Talent Publishing Editor

INTRODUCTION
WHY WILD WEALTH?

Rich people aren't always the rich people. Wealth and how people define wealth is evolving and this book is the next step in that evolution. Even our publisher didn't quite understand our definition of wealth in the beginning. I can't say that's rare. The simple truth is that most people don't really understand what to value and treasure. I'll tell you what true wealth is but let first let me tell you what it's not.

Wealth isn't necessarily money in the bank, 401K's, real estate, crypto currency, mutual funds, stocks or even owning your own business. Yes, all these things have value, but these ideas of wealth are more than a little obvious. They are also somewhat one-dimensional and limited by today's new way of viewing wealth. Some of you are probably thinking that the wealth I am referring to is time and freedom but even those are somewhat obvious answers, and I am truly not trying to be clever.

So, the highest and truest wealth isn't as simple as cash, crypto, and real estate and it isn't as over-simplistic as time and freedom. Nowadays more than ever, wealth is access and leverage and all the ways in which that shows up in the world. This includes everything from your mindset to mentors. The wealthiest people have access to everything from backstage passes with the biggest talent to doctors with the most advanced treatments. The wealthiest people have leverage in the world that include everything from hard-to-get resources to patented technology to priceless experiences.

> *"If you want to see how wealthy you really are just count all the things you have that money can't buy."*
>
> - UNKNOWN

Hammer and Nails

This book has rounded up an influential group of women that are wealthy in more ways than one. Their stories speak to the power of access, leverage, mindset, perspective, mentors, prosperity, mastery, and more. We call them women gone wild because they unapologetically live life on their terms. They value collecting moments not things and in their own way are moment millionaires. This isn't to say that they don't have traditional assets, many do, but beyond those material possessions, they have something more.

Real wealth is knowing that you could lose all your material possessions and that you could make it all back if that's what mattered most to you. A wealthy woman is one that could be picked up and dropped off in a new place in a new industry and they could rise to the top again because of their wild ways. Wild women don't play by the rules rather we bend them and break them at will for a greater cause.

You can have all the time and freedom you want but real wealth is more than even these things because real wealth is enjoying true treasure that comes from access, leverage, and love for what matters most in this journey we call life.

Welcome to *Women Gone Wild the Wealth Edition*. Prepare to make progress in the world of prosperity and wealth.

Sincerely,

RHONDA SWAN

01

BRAND CURRENCY OWNS THE CROWN

BY RHONDA SWAN

"When the tide goes out, you know who's been swimming naked."

- WARREN BUFFET

You can't skip the introduction. Read it twice because it's the foundation for the fortune of wisdom accumulated in this book. You can now build on your new definition of wealth with this chapter about credit... however, it's not what you think, I can guarantee it. You're going to hear this a lot in this book because so much of true wealth is a shift in thinking and believing. It's the redefining of how you look at wealth or any of the topics shared.

For example, when most people think of credit, they are thinking about credit bureau agencies like Experian, Equifax, and TransUnion for personal credit or Dun and Bradstreet for business credit but that's mainstream game playing.

Brand Currency is the real game-changer that gives you real access and leverage.

Your track record of success, reputation and list of accomplishments and overall brand positioning is the strongest and most long-lasting currency you can have anywhere in the world. I have personally leveraged investment capital based on my name alone and no one ever pulled a credit report. I have accessed opportunities that ended up being priceless and I never filled out any kind of application. Rather it was my brand and reputation for getting results that opened doors for me. You too can have Brand Currency, if you know how to build it.

When The Tide Goes Out

The moment COVID hit the world freaked and business owners started to scramble to get online if they hadn't already been set up to function this way.

I remember the moment, it was March 14th, 2020, I was at dinner with my husband (Brian) and a friend. We were at a new trendy restaurant that just opened near Canggu beach in Bali. "Penny Lanes" the place was full of people despite the announcement that the USA was going into lockdown. The three of us were discussing what was happening in the world, and how none of these people had any clue about what was about to happen in the world. The topic of discussion was the headline that popped up on our phone from CNN "The NBA has canceled March Madness" and the season will be canceled until further notice.

Here we sat at this table looking at each other in disbelief "This is getting real" our friend said. The world is about to change. But the three of us sat there with calmness and trust discussing our next best moves because over the last 15 years we had been building our brands, and business structures completely online. At that moment my favorite quote came to mind:

> *"When the tide goes out, you know who's been swimming naked."*
>
> ### - WARREN BUFFET

I remember reading this from Warren Buffet many years back, and today it was clearer than ever. "Many people will be revealed, if they haven't prepared themselves," I said.

What Warren Buffet is talking about is those who look good on the outside but haven't set themselves up properly in any market will find themselves exposed when it comes down to the real truth behind their success.

This is where true Brand Currency comes from and if you're not building it, there is no more time to wait.

Don't Take My Word for It

Brand Currency could be made up of testimonials, endorsements, before and after pictures, proof of results, or even social proof. This kind of rewarding reputation is based on your list of accomplishments and your ability to make things happen in the world. The closest most

people get to this is with their CV's or resumes.
It's only the tip of the iceberg with 90 percent of the mass underneath the waterline out of sight.

"If you build it, they will come."

- FIELD OF DREAMS

In 2004, I made the decision to quit my corporate job so that I could raise a family. We had just bought a 5-bedroom home in San Diego, California so when I came home and told Brian I was quitting my job and starting a business online, he almost passed out. "I don't care if you're my boss's, boss's, boss, I'll never make enough money to cover the mortgage of this house on my salary," he said.

"I'm going to work online," I told him. I had just finished watching a documentary where Steve Jobs said, "If you don't learn how to leverage the internet, in 10 years you'll be left in the dark." And that's exactly what I did, I started to learn online branding, google ad words, SEO, and market targeting.

From Quitting to Thriving

I not only quit my corporate job, but I retired Brian as a robotics engineer in the first year of building my business and brand online. Going from being a corporate executive for a Fortune 100 company to an online brand expert shook some heads. My boss told me she would hold my position because she knew I'd come back. That was over 18 years ago, and I've never looked back.

My focus was on teaching people how to build their online brand, by defining their message, image, and strategy and how to connect with their audience using SEO and Google Ads.

Then once social media came out the possibilities opened even more doors for others to be successful at building their online presence and brand.

In the last 15 years, I've helped build over 1,000 new brands, products, and businesses for others, and have written over 15 books and manuals showing others how to brand themselves.

Even greater accomplishments that are respected and admired in today's world are publishing a bestselling book, being featured in the media, or speaking in front of audiences -both quality and in quantity. These things are so valuable that my whole business has been dedicated to branding people, publishing people, and publicizing them.

Brands that don't embrace digital PR strategies lose ground on their competitors. Not only do they struggle to compete, but they may threaten their very existence. Done right, digital PR can set your brand on fire in people's hearts and minds.

Can't Be Stolen

The truth is that this kind of brand currency is what can make someone the type of wealth that can never truly be taken away. You can do everything from attracting investment capital to celebrity involvement with nothing but your brand currency. This book series has done just that for me. Because of my access to the media and speaking platforms, I have influence and that access and influence is a significant part of the new definition of wealth.

When we decided to launch the first book "Women Gone Wild", it was a passion project to help more women share their voices and be heard. But after the success and the feedback we got from the first book becoming a Best Seller in multiple categories on Amazon and capturing the awareness of several celebrities and influential women we decided to launch the W.I.L.D. series.

W- Wealth (the book you're reading)

I- Intuition

L-Leadership

D- Diversity

This book became a brand, that had a heartbeat, a message, and an audience that wanted to know more and be part of the movement. We had over 3 million viewers on our first WGW summit, of people sharing the message which caught the eye of publications like *Forbes magazine, Hollywood Digest and USA Today.*

Every woman aligned with this book was able to leverage the brand currency for their own credibility and recognition.

You want to have such a great reputation that even if someone was to say something bad about you no one would believe them. That's wealth. You want to have so much brand currency that even if you temporarily had a poor credit rating people would still invest in you. That's wealth and it's available to everyone willing to live their lives with fulfilling purpose and meaningful intention.

Obey The PR Golden Rule: ABR

At its heart, Public Relations & Branding are about building and managing relationships. We follow the ABR rule for successful PR & Brand Building.

Always Build Relationships

Start and strengthen relationships with customers, peers, influencers, or journalists, always. You won't go wrong if you build relationships everywhere, with everyone, every time. Powerful relationships with all stakeholders make it easier for you to shape public perceptions of your brand.

Think about this for a moment

Powerful connections with customers mean they will be loyal to your brand and tell their friends about you (free word-of-mouth marketing). Good relationships with journalists mean they will gladly cover your brand or pick you over another brand for a mention. Favorable relationships with the community mean they will back you during a crisis.

Beneficial relationships with peers in your niche mean they will support all your branding initiatives. Good relationships are the linchpin of positive perspectives about your brand. It's never too late or too early to build relationships with all stakeholders who are key to the growth of your brand.

So, build relationships—now and forever. Your brand will be better for it.

-Rhonda Swan

Rhonda Swan is the CEO of the *Unstoppable Branding Agency* and was rated by *Forbes* as the Top Branding & PR Firm for Entrepreneurs in 2021. They work with CEOs, executives, and entrepreneurs to create a defined google footprint, using CELEBRITY branding & top-tier PR & media. After spending nearly a decade working in PR and marketing for fortune 100 companies & multimillion-dollar brands, Rhonda knows what truly drives conversions, sold-out launches, and how to get her clients featured in top-tier publications like *Forbes, INC, Entrepreneur, and USA Today.* Rhonda has landed coverage in print and broadcast outlets around the world, being featured on the *Adam Carolla Show, Good Morning America, ABC News, Forbes, Entrepreneur, INC. Success, & Business Insider.* In addition to her role as a CEO, she also hosts the *Rhonda Swan Show* and has interviewed celebrity names like Grant Cardone, Elena Cardone, Diana Wentworth, Patti Negri (celebrity medium), and John Lee Dumas, and NFL fullback

Chris Gronkowski. She is also the author of the best-selling book series *Women Gone Wild: The Feminine Guide to Fearless Living.*

02

WHAT YOU VALUE

BY HANALEI SWAN

*"Do what you love, and success will follow. Passion
is the fuel behind a successful career."*

- MEG WHITMAN

How do you define wealth? Does wealth come from
the money you make, the things you can buy, or the
things that you own? One of the many definitions of
wealth is a plentiful supply of particularly desirable
things. So, with that definition, wealth can subjectively be
anything that holds value to a particular person. One of
the things I find most valuable in life is creating memories
and experiences.

I wrote one day, "Someday this moment will fade
away; the seconds we are living now will become only a
memory to us. When we toil in the future or the past we
forget about the present and waste the only seconds on
this earth we are truly guaranteed: the moments we are
living now."

Ever since I was one year old, I've grown up traveling the world with my family. This way of life started when my parents lost everything in the 07- 08 real estate crash. Instead of going back to their corporate jobs, they decided to start working online and create a business virtually (when the internet was just starting to become a thing), while traveling the world with the little money they had. We would usually never stay in one place longer than six months at a time.

I've traveled to six continents and over 24 countries in the last 15 years, bouncing from school to school and making new friends along the way. Growing up, I never placed a lot of value on material things, usually having to give away all my belongings every time we moved. To me, the things that held the most value in my life were my memories; something irreplaceable, something I could never give away.

Mind Captures

From a young age, I learned that the value of being present and capturing these important moments meant more to me than anything I could buy. When I was young, before I started to use a phone, I remember trying to take photos with my mind. I would stare at something beautiful for a long time, like a sunset, and then close my eyes fast and try to paint the picture again in my head. I used to believe if I did that then I would remember it forever.

Growing up I became obsessed with creating these memories and staying present, doing anything I could to capture these moments. One of the most important things I heard growing up was, "We never know when our expiration date may be." That single sentence has stuck with me for life, a reminder that nothing is permanent.

A time will come when we must depart from this Earth. This knowledge shouldn't come with fear but should instead come as a reminder to do what makes you happy and live the way you want to every single day. We dwell so much on the past with regrets and worry about the future that we often forget to just live in the present. Ever since I was young, life was all about being happy and enjoying the moments I'm able to spend on this Earth. Whenever someone asked me, "What do you want to be when you grow up?" I'd always respond with, "Happy, I want to be happy, no matter where I end up in life." That statement still rings true to this day.

Dad's memories

I was always fascinated with reminiscing, spending so much time with my dad, and asking him repeatedly to tell me a new surf story or an interesting tidbit from when he was my age.

He had so many memories that would captivate me for hours on end; I always wanted to be like both of my parents, great storytellers. Those moments together watching the sunset with my dad and listening to him until dark made me want to one day have worthy and exciting enough stories in my life to pass down to others.

The stories of my mom and dad's past taught me so much, especially my dad's story starting with the statement, "We never know when our expiration date may be."

As my dad was growing up, he knew his father was sick. Their family never talked about it, but in the back of their minds, they always knew. When my dad was 6 years old, his mother and father got divorced and Dad found out his dad was gay. The sickness my grandfather had was AIDS, and at the time it was something that no one understood, and a virus with no known cure.

Flipped Switch

My grandfather went from a hard-working entrepreneur to someone who came to realize they had an expiration date; the doctors said he would probably have less than a year to live. It was almost like a switch flipped inside of his mind. One day, he asked my dad and his siblings if anyone wanted to go on a trip.

Over the next 5 years, my grandfather took my uncle, aunt, and my dad across the world, showing them a completely new perspective compared to their farm town life. They got to see their dad live out his bucket list while being with them.

My grandfather passed away when my dad was 16. Even though I never got to meet him, my grandfather has had such a huge impact on my life; inspiring my dad 25 years later to travel the world again with his family. My dad gave me similar experiences to what his dad gave him when he was my age.

Why You Would

The reason I'm telling you this is because your cherished memories and highest values can be a guide for the best ways to be wealthy in life. You might be wondering, why would you listen to me, out of all the inspiring people in the world or in this book? When I was 11 years old, I started my first company after being asked the simple question, "What do you want to be now?" instead of the usual, "What do you want to be when you grow up?" This very question helped me realize that living my passion and dreams is what creates wealth.

When I was first starting my company, my main goal was never to make money or become rich from my business selling eco-friendly fashion. I wanted to accumulate experiences and knowledge from running a small company, and most importantly, live by my highest value, which was creating things that I loved, while being able to share them with the world. I hope to inspire people to do what they love now by showing people it's possible to do anything, no matter your age.

So why do adults so often get hung up on the question, "Are you living the life you wanted to be living when you were a kid?" (Are you living the life you've always dreamed of?) Because most people nowadays probably aren't. When you were a kid you probably never said you wanted to be in an office all day or stressed out about whenever life throws a curveball your way.

Reflect On

This is your reminder to do what you love and what gives you the most joy. But doing what you love every day, is probably a lot easier said than done. It takes time to really come to yourself and reflect on what you want to change in your life to make it ideal for you.

Are you being influenced by others' perceptions of what your life should be? Are you currently following the social norm? Are you truly doing what you love now? People's visions and perceptions of us can regularly influence how we present ourselves, often leading to us making life choices that we really don't want, but what we think we "should do" so we try our best to fit inside this box, just like everybody else.

Highest Values

Ask yourself, am I really doing what I love? Am I happy with the current life I am living? If there is a hesitation while you're asking yourself these questions, maybe it's time to make a shift.

Something that helped me figure out what I really love to do, was writing down what gives me the most joy in my life. Things that I could wake up every single day and do without anyone telling me I needed to do it. These are your highest values.

My parents taught me when I was young that to make money, you don't need to fall into the system of going to college and working a nine-to-five job just to make ends meet.

I learned that there was a way to make money from your passions and by doing what you love.

But it can't be as easy as following a checklist; becoming an entrepreneur is not a one-way nonstop train. It's like hiking an open trail with thousands of different paths and outcomes, you must find your own way, what works for you, and trust the process along the way.

What path do you want to follow? The first step to do anything is always and literally taking the first step. This could be writing out your intentions of what you want in life, reaching out to people that can help you, researching, etc., but the first step can only and must always come from you.

Heart Lit

You know what they say, "The Journey of a Thousand Miles starts with a single step." This is your call to start your journey, in any direction it may be, in your business, your social life, hobbies, free time, wherever you want to take your life, this is your life, no one else's. The most important thing is doing what lights up your heart.

Remember to stay present and use the time you have to the fullest, these moments will one day become memories, so you might as well make them worth remembering.

So, if you knew you had an expiration date, what would you do?

-Hanalei Swan

Hanalei Swan is a 15-year-old fashion designer, artist, model, international speaker, and author. At the age of 7, her talents were discovered and the journey began. Her parents never asked her "What do you want to be when you grow up?" they asked her "What do you want to be, NOW!?" This started her career as a fashion designer and today Hanalei is one of the youngest fashion designers and business owners in the world, producing high-fashion life & earth-conscious products out of her showroom in Bali, Indonesia. She has spoken on stages in Australia, Hong Kong, India, London, USA - Las Vegas & Orlando, and Indonesia. She also released her book *How to Be & Raise an UNSTOPPABLE Kid* in January 2019, and is also a contributing author of the best-selling book series *Women Gone Wild*.

03

ЄxPЄCT MAGIC!

BY DIANA VON WELANETZ
WENTWORTH

*The world is full of magic things, patiently waiting
for our senses to grow sharper.*

- W B YEATS

Are you feeling it? The power, the passion, the exuberance of feminine energy?

Women won't keep a lid on wildness anymore.

We ask ourselves daily what will bring us and those around us the most joy and fulfillment. We ask what we can grow into. We welcome new directions into our brightest possible futures.

Expecting magic, we trust when it appears!

I shall tell you the story of how magically my own life has evolved, and how it continues to expand. Even at eighty! Even though recently widowed a second time.

As a child I found myself living in a serious world! Dinner table discussions were ominous. Children should be seen and not heard. Be a lady!

While I marveled at coincidences, serendipity, signs of invisible support, I was cautioned to be careful and "get real." But a small precious part of me was always irrepressible. No one could keep a lid on me for long. At eight, I was sent away to a girls' boarding school. I was lonely there. There were very few boarders, none my age.

Wounds Birth Wisdom

That deep loneliness, though a wound, would serve me well. More than anything in the world, even as a young girl, I yearned for a future romantic partner who would be my forever love. I sensed how fulfilling deep intimacy would feel. I just knew I would find a way to share my whole heart.

Meanwhile, I noticed how I loved to delight people. Whenever I lit up someone's day, my own brightened. I used many techniques – practical jokes, riddles, humor, and magic tricks to lighten up my serious family.

Most delightful to me was cooking. My mother and her mother, who ran a boarding house, spent lots of time in the kitchen. What warmth, fun, and generosity they shared while preparing delicious food! I loved being in the kitchen with them, perusing recipes, planning menus, and preparing treats. The most fun was anticipating what pleasure it would bring. Chopping and prepping, sautéing, and simmering, I was stirring blessings into every bite.

Occasionally, suddenly and shockingly, I sensed an event that had yet to happen. I called it Inner Knowing.

In the spring of 1959, my sorority sisters and I were sprawled on the porch. I asked someone to turn the music down.

"Oh, Diana doesn't like Elvis Presley!"

"Actually, I do like him, and I'm going to date him someday!"

Where did that come from? I wondered. Of course, they laughed at me.

A few months later, my mother took me on a "Cook's Tour" of Europe that began at the Hotel Prince De Galles, in Paris. Bobbie, a young boy on our tour, ran up to me as I entered the lobby.

"Elvis is in the dining room! I'm scared to ask him for an autograph!"

"Come with me!" I proclaimed.

Drop-dead gorgeous in his Army uniform, his blue eyes lit up as I approached. Charming and courteous, he took Bobbie's pen and signed. He told us he was on his first leave from the Army, visiting Paris for the first time. That very evening, my mother and I attended an early show at the Moulin Rouge and Elvis was in the audience. Afterward, back at the hotel, he was waiting in the lobby when our tour bus returned. He stood up and invited my mother to join him. He asked how she was enjoying Paris and then asked if he might escort me to the Lido Nightclub for the late show.

Why me? Perhaps he needed a girl on his arm because the press had been alerted. For whatever reason, I was his date, thrilled to be with him. Later, in his room, he played the guitar and sang the theme from Moulin Rouge for this audience of one.

I know what you're wondering. Yes, we kissed.

Another meeting that felt magically destined occurred three years later in Hong Kong. At the age of twenty-one, I felt another knowing. Without warning, I broke up with the approved "eligible bachelor" I'd been dating, and at the last minute tagged along with my parents on their long-planned tour of Asia.

For the next three weeks, as we visited Japan, the Philippines, Vietnam, and Cambodia, I was sure I'd made the right decision. While enjoying this world travel, I also felt a quiet sense of anticipation. Hong Kong was our final stop. I didn't even notice that a man in the dining room had followed me to the elevator, only to have it close in his face. I woke very early the next morning, way too early to meet my parents for breakfast. Yet I chose an elegant dress to wear as if for a special occasion, went downstairs, and stood in the middle of the lobby.

What am I doing here so early? Paul von Welanetz stepped out of the elevator, and I found out.

"Where are you from?" With those words, my longed-for heart's companion had arrived. Three days later we were engaged.

Feeling our Way into Our Future

Our truly romantic marriage lasted twenty-five years, and what a fabulous and fun career we shared and built together! I'd always loved cooking; gathering people around the table to enjoy each other made my heart sing. Thanks to Julia Child, a massive interest in French cooking and entertaining took hold in America. I loved learning, and during the first years of our marriage, I attended classes with the head chef of the Escoffier Room in Beverly Hills.

Paul, an artist at heart, loved to present food and table decor in imaginative ways. He would quote Mies van der Rohe: "First you eat with your eyes!"

Our shared passion began with cooking classes in our home and grew into a groundbreaking career in cooking and entertaining. Our first book, *ThePleasure of your Company*, won the French Tastemaker "Cookbook of the Year" Award in the category of entertaining.

Five more books followed, along with our cooking school on the Sunset Strip, where Wolfgang Puck and other rising chefs taught. *Los Angeles Magazine* featured Paul and me as one of L.A.'s most romantic couples. We even hosted an early television cooking show on the Lifetime Network, *The New Way Gourmet*. And then, as happens with trends, it all fell apart. By 1985, women entered the workforce in droves and lost interest in spending hours at the stove.

Challenged to Reinvent our Career

Paul and I were feeling pressured. We couldn't and didn't think of a way other than cooking to make a living. Paul searched the want ads. I worried and paced the floor, impatient to know NOW what our new direction could be.

Out of desperation, alone in the bedroom, I asked out loud for our next step. A few years earlier, when we'd been waiting too long to be offered our own TV show, I'd done the same thing. "Give us a show now!" I had demanded. Within hours, we were offered our own show on two different networks.

Please take note: Erupting wildness must be honored and amplified to its full force. Add fierceness, not polite pleas, to your prayers! Even though I recognized this at the time, it never really sank in until the launch of *Women Gone Wild*.

A Whole New Tribe!

Paul and I had always found ourselves drawn toward

personal growth. We both meditated, attended lectures and workshops, and read avidly.

We committed to the cost of "Impact," a motivational seminar for people in the entertainment industry. One of the many challenges was the unusual meeting times – daily 6 to 8 a.m., and most full weekends! Our nine-month stint was life-changing. Several hundred of us were coaxed into setting nearly impossible goals and were held accountable to achieve them. "Your considerations don't count. All that counts is the action you take!"

As we focused on action, magic multiplied. Other participants, such as Jack Canfield, Dr. Barbara DeAngelis, and others who were just launching their careers also experienced amazing results.

Through association with Impact, Paul and I were invited to travel to the Soviet Union at the height of the Cold War to be part of a documentary on "Citizen Diplomacy." We were to somehow create dialogues and connections with Soviet citizens at a time when our respective government diplomats were not speaking. Our situation was terrifying. Our rooms were bugged. Soviet police barged into our cabins on trains and tore through our luggage, confiscating anything they considered propaganda. Our motives were questioned every day. We hardly slept. At the same time, we gained an appreciation for observing and listening to our fellow travelers, who were activists and leaders in human potential, including Dennis Weaver, Barbara Marx Hubbard, author Alan Cohen, Mike Farrell from *MASH*,

Swami Satchidananda, and the real Patch Adams. We marveled at how the group rallied support for our cause. We felt more and more empowered, and made what would become lifelong connections.

Breakthrough!

What if we don't need to prepare food in order to gather people together? After that trip, Paul and I wondered how to create delight in others on a grander scale by offering larger, more meaningful gatherings in restaurants. Power breakfasts and networking were just beginning in New York.

Hopping early onto the next trend, Paul and I used our hosting skills to produce phenomenal events.

The Inside Edge, a weekly breakfast in three Southern California cities, was launched. Those weekly breakfasts at the Beverly Hills Hotel, with compelling speakers, caught on. The Inside Edge spread, attracting folks who had not yet written books but were to become famous. Our first speaker was futurist Barbara Marx Hubbard. Paul and I also hosted imaginative, challenging parties for our members.

Stay in Character

"Come as you will be in five years!" The rule was that you had to stay in character throughout and tell everyone what you had achieved. Dr. Susan Jeffers stepped out of a limousine holding three mock books and announced that she had just returned from her third New York Times bestseller tour. Her first book, *Feel the Fear and Do It*

Anyway, soon became a massive bestseller, followed by two more. She achieved what she'd announced! And so did others. The Law of Attraction, of creating vivid feelings before achieving what you wish for, was standard practice at The Inside Edge. Many of the world's most successful authors and motivational speakers gave talks at our meetings. Attendees still speak of how uplifting and magical it felt to step into that meeting room at 6:30 a.m.

Magic continued to manifest through us and all those around us. I was learning to expect it! Recently, at the Inside Edge 35th Anniversary Gala in 2021, Jack Canfield acknowledged that he had used our "five years ahead" party at the conclusion of every training he has done since. He also remarked that without the Inside Edge, *Chicken Soup for the Soul*, the largest selling book series of all time (half a billion sold!), may never have come into being.

A New Love

Paul, just after our 25th anniversary in 1989, was diagnosed with terminal cancer. He surprised me by saying, "I don't want you to be alone."

"Send me someone!" I blurted.

"I will!"

He did. Ted Wentworth walked right into my life and my heart at the Inside Edge, bringing me thirty-one more years of marital bliss. My romantic memoir, "Send

Me Someone: A True Story of Love Here and Hereafter"
tells the story. Though I deeply miss Ted's affection, his
encouragement, his playful wit, I now savor solitude—and
an entirely new sense of sovereignty to explore.

Real Magic!

Here I am, almost eighty-one, widowed for the second
time, not just expecting, but being flooded with more
magic than ever! You see, now that I'm alone, I don't
really need to behave myself. I can loudly insist on magic!
Order in a miracle! How it works, I don't know. What I do
know is my inner knowing loves to be called upon. And
trusted!

Less than a year ago, I'd just blurted something
revealing and perhaps disgraceful to a large group
online. There was a certain giddiness that I felt through
my embarrassment. I identified it as trapped exuberance
finding its voice. I had an idea to purchase the domain
www.womenwritingwild.com.

A few weeks later I was coincidently invited to write the
Foreword for the first edition of this Women Gone Wild
book series. With that instant bestseller came a global
sisterhood. It's non-stop now.

Wild energy goes on and on!

Most empowering of all is my discovery of a most
magical tool! NuCalm, a phone app that provides a drug-
free way to control brain waves and choose a desired
mental state is helping me live joyful and creative days!

While listening to music, I find myself floating in a blissful space of wonder. I invite guidance. Where can I inspire the most joy today? What magical step lies ahead? How wildly wonderful can my life become?

Try it, and…Expect Magic!

-Diana von Welanetz Wentworth

For over 3 decades, Diana von Welanetz Wentworth has been the Founder and Program Director of the *Inside Edge* which was designed to inspire the next generation of thought leaders at a weekly breakfast forum in Southern California that helped launch the careers of many of the most celebrated authors and speakers of our day like Jack Canfield, Barbara De Angelis, John Gray, Barbara Marx Hubbard, Louise Hay, and many others at the start of their careers.

Diana is the author of several best-selling and award-winning books like *Chicken Soup for the Soul Cookbook: 101 Stories with Recipes from the Heart, Send Me Someone: A True Story of Love Here and Hereafter, The Von Welanetz Guide to Ethnic Ingredients: How to Buy and Prepare More Than 1,000 Foods from Around the World, The Pleasure of Your Company* and the co-author of two Chicken Soup for the Soul titles. *The rights to her book Send Me Someone: A True Story of Love Here and Hereafter* were purchased by the Lifetime Network, and *The Pleasure of Your Company* was the recipient of the Cookbook of the Year award. Diana has done everything from hosting her own tv show to being an international keynote speaker at women's meetings, writer's conferences, and on cruise ships. She is a certified life coach who specializes in reinvention.

With her business partner Robin Mullin, she launched *Wisdom Cirlces*, which provides women of exceptional mastery ongoing meetings with peers to explore feminine subjects including reinvention, legacy, and the highest potential for their personal "Encore."

Diana offers private coaching. Two new books are in the works along with a video podcast, *Encore!*, featuring many of the most inspiring and influential authors and speakers she has hosted.

04
ABUNDANT LIVING

BY DANA KAY

"It is health that is real wealth and not pieces of gold or silver."

- MAHATMA GANDHI

My life was a mess. I knew it. My husband knew it. And on this particular day, everyone at Costco in Seattle, Washington, knew it too.

"But I don't want to wait!" My eldest son, Oliver, held a box of crackers in his hands, trying to open the top before I could snatch it away. We were in the freezer aisle, and I was almost finished with my grocery list. I could see the exit doors right ahead. So close.

"Just a little bit longer," I told him. "We're almost done. Once we've paid for them, you can have as many as you want." I hoped—naively—that this promise would hold him over.

But deep down, I knew what was coming next. This wasn't my first rodeo.

I Held My Breath

Oliver threw himself onto the supermarket floor.

"*I want it now!*" he screamed, flailing his limbs like a completely out-of-control octopus. I watched in horror as his legs neared a spaghetti sauce endcap. One foot hit a jar of sauce and sent it flying onto the floor. Glass shattered. Sauce splattered everywhere. My face grew hot and turned red from embarrassment.

That's when I heard a comment from a young, pregnant woman in high heels standing a few feet away. "I'm never going to let my kid do *that*," she whispered to her friend standing beside her. They both shook their heads and then looked away.

You might be wondering why I'm sharing such an embarrassing story. I'm sharing it because I imagine you've had days like this too, days when you wished you could disappear.

My Big Wish

My big wish that day was to escape my life. Have you ever felt like this? Have you ever wanted to run away from your life?

On that day, I didn't want to deal with my son's tantrums anymore. I didn't want to walk on eggshells, waiting for the next meltdown. I didn't want to feel judged every time we left the house because of my son's behavior.

I wanted happiness. Peace. Joy. Wealth.

Not money wealth–though of course that would be nice too–but more than that, I wanted abundant life wealth. I wanted to actually enjoy my life. Since you're reading this book, you probably want some of these things too, but maybe you think they're too far out of reach. That's how I felt back then also.

That night, I went home and told my husband, Ben, "Honestly, I don't even like my own child."

Of course, I loved him. But I didn't like him, not when his behavior was so challenging. Still, what kind of mother actually says those words out loud?

Something had to change, but I never expected our entire lives to be turned upside down.

The Wrong Person

The next day I made a phone call to my son's doctor. Shortly after that, we went in for an evaluation, and Ollie was diagnosed with attention deficit hyperactivity disorder (ADHD). His doctor handed me a prescription and sent us on our way. He didn't tell us about any other options besides medicine, so I did what any other parent in my situation would likely do. I listened to his advice.

When Oliver had side effects from that medication, and the doctor suggested adding a second and then a third, I listened again. He was the expert, after all. Who was I to suggest anything different from what the expert was saying?

I'll tell you who. I'm Oliver's mom. I'm the person who probably knows him better than anyone else. I should have listened to my gut when those medications weren't working for him. I should have trusted myself more than I trusted someone else.

I Finally Stopped

When that same doctor suggested the fourth medication for my young son–exclusively to manage side effects caused by the other three–I finally stopped listening to him and started listening to the voice inside telling me enough was enough.

Have you ever heard that inner voice telling you what to do next? Maybe you've spent years hushing it, forcing it to quiet down, assuming it didn't know what was best for you. When I finally started listening to my inner voice, my entire life trajectory changed.

It Changed Everything

I started looking into alternative ADHD treatments that didn't require multiple prescriptions with side effects we couldn't ignore. I learned about the gut-brain connection.

The foods we eat can affect every area of our lives, from emotional regulation, mood, and behavior to ADHD symptoms and a host of other areas that might not seem to be related to food but are. Food is powerful, and the more I learned, the more I changed our family's diet.

Slowly, my son's behavior began to change. We stopped dreading each day and began to enjoy our time together. We got off the emotional rollercoaster we'd been on for years. Tantrums used to be daily but were happening less and less.

As I continued to adjust our diet—getting rid of inflammatory foods and providing nutrient-dense whole foods instead—symptoms that used to bear down on our entire family began to fall by the wayside. My son's ADHD symptoms stopped controlling him, and he became the child I always knew he could be.

The Ripple Effect

When Oliver was diagnosed with ADHD, I worked in business and accounting. I assumed that's where I would stay. But the more I learned about the effects of food on children with ADHD and other similar disorders, the more I felt pulled in another direction.

You might feel pulled in another direction too. It can be hard to change. I've been there.

But after witnessing the transforming power of food with my own eyes, how could I not share this information with others?

I couldn't.

I went back to school and became a Board-Certified Holistic Health and Nutrition Practitioner, opened a practice, and began helping other parents of children with ADHD.

Medication isn't bad and has its place, but it's not always the right solution for every child.

Today so much of the medical world takes a cookie-cutter approach: if a patient has X, they get Y. There's very little personalization involved.

This Needs to Change

Parents need to know they have options besides a prescription. If a medication causes side effects or if a family does not want to go down that pharmaceutical route, there are alternatives that are just as effective—and at times, even more effective. It's possible to find relief from ADHD symptoms without popping a pill. Parents need to know this information, and I decided I would be one of the people to tell them.

Over time that decision led to a ripple effect. What started as just one person has now grown and spread. As more people learn, they teach those around them, expanding the ripple exponentially.

No More Dread

I don't dread my day-to-day life anymore. Do you dread yours? I've been there, and I know how hard that can be. I also know it doesn't have to stay that way.

In fact, I'm now living that abundant life I always thought was out of reach, in large part because my son's ADHD symptoms are gone. He isn't on any medications and is doing better without them than he ever did with them.

But there's another reason I'm living the abundant life, something that has nothing to do with my son's behavior and everything to do with my career.

Now I'm not working solely for a paycheck; I'm working in my passion and helping other families do the same. I'm living the life I was meant to live.

You might not be able to imagine living a life of passion, enjoying each day, and looking forward to the future, but it's possible for you too.

Keys to Abundant Living

That grocery store trip turned out to be the best thing that ever happened to me because it was the triggering event that led to everything I'm doing now.

I don't know why you picked up this book on wild, wealthy living, but I do know this: you picked it up because you were meant to read it.

Something inside needed to read the stories within the pages of this book. Maybe you picked it up because you want to live an abundant life, too. Maybe you're wondering how that's even possible based on your current circumstances. Looking at life today, maybe you can't imagine it ever being any different, any better. I want you to know it can be.

Abundant living isn't nearly as far off as it might seem. It all begins by doing the following three things.

Key One: Listen to the right people

More than anything else, listening to the right people means listening to *yourself*, trusting your instincts, and quieting the inner critic that says you're wrong. It means ignoring the naysayers who disagree with you. It means that if someone tells you to do something you don't think is the right thing, you don't have to listen to them.

You might have been told you wasted your life. I know I wasted months of my life battling side effects caused by medication that I knew in my gut was not what my son needed. That's not to say medication is not right for you or your family. You must trust *your* gut, whatever it is telling you. My only regret is not listening to my instincts sooner. I hope you'll listen to yours.

Living an abundant life begins by listening to yourself!

Key Two: Find your passion

When I was working in business and accounting, I worked for a paycheck. I enjoyed things about my job and the people who worked there, but it wasn't my passion. It was a means to an end. I was making a living but not enjoying life.

`If you're not loving what you're doing, then maybe you shouldn't be doing it. Find your passion. Live your dream life. Don't settle for just making a paycheck. Life is more than money, and wealth is more than having cash in a bank account. True wealth is living your dream life—in abundance, in passion, in joy.

Key Three: Share your passion

I get so much joy from helping other families find the same freedom from ADHD symptoms that my family has found. One of the children we worked with used to eat only five total foods, but now he eats more than one hundred. He used to have daily rage episodes, but those are non-existent now that his family has changed how they eat.

Another child used to get in trouble constantly at school. One year he and his brother had thirty-seven total suspensions. The next year, once his mom learned the powerful effects of food and changed their diets, these children had zero suspensions. In fact, they even won awards at school for their good behavior.

Helping these people didn't only help them. It also blessed me!

When we give to others out of our passion, we are blessed in return. The universe, a higher power, God—

whatever you believe in—does not give us gifts so that we can hoard them for ourselves but so that we can share them for the greater good.

If you want to live an abundant life, listen to the voice that matters most: yours. Find your passion. Then share that passion with the world around you. Our gifts are meant to be shared with those around us, and *that*, my friends, is when abundant living really begins.

-Dana Kay

Dana Kay is a Board-Certified Holistic Health and Nutrition Practitioner and the founder of *The ADHD Thrive Method 4 Kids* program. As a mother of a child with ADHD, she knows firsthand the struggles that come with parenting a neurodiverse child, but she also knows the freedom that is possible once parents learn to reduce ADHD symptoms. Dana has been featured in *Forbes, Authority Magazine, Medium, Influencive, Thrive Global*, and various others. She has also been a guest on multiple parenting and ADHD summits and podcasts. Her mission is to help families reduce ADHD symptoms naturally so that children with ADHD can thrive at home, at school, and in life.

05

AUDIENCE CURRENCY

BY ISABEL FAGAN

"It's not what you know, it's not even who you know rather it's who knows you."

- UNKNOWN

Exposure is a form of wealth. Access to an audience is good but having your own audience is best. Some people from the past would call this their golden rolodex but nowadays we refer to this more as our following. This includes things like your list of email/text opt-in's, LinkedIn connections, Instagram followers, Facebook friends, YouTube subscribers, platform members, or event registrants.

The Making of a Movement

These people we have permission to communicate with are in fact what I call audience currency. Not only can a big audience translate into big money it can translate into a big movement. People will pay good money and priceless favors for access to your influence in your audience. Love them or not Oprah Winfrey, Tom

Brady, Howard Stern, Serena Williams, Donald Trump, Kim Kardashian, the Dalai Lama, and the Pope have a significant following. In many cases, the audiences these famous figures have are significant and priceless to a lot of people.

The power of an audience goes beyond any one person as well. There are elite country clubs, insider opportunities in IVY league alumni, and Hall of Famer's alike that provide lucrative access. Just look at the Academy, AARP, NRA, United Nations, or even the Red Cross. Media outlets like F*ox News, CNN, NY Times, Forbes, Bloomberg, Los Angeles Tribune, Vogue, Cosmopolitan, Rolling Stone, GQ*, and *Time* all have significant reach. It's because of their audiences they are the influential juggernauts they are.

Rhonda Swan, the driving force behind this book, has a million Instagram followers. My average Top Talent Magazine issue has close to 200,000 impressions. The co-authors in this book have a combined reach in the hundreds of millions.

So, what are you doing to expand your audience and build your golden rolodex? Access to your very own audience puts you in a position of power. It's a total paradigm shift of prosperity. Do you want to be the person constantly asking for favors and buying access to other people's audiences or would you like to flip the script and be the person being asked for access? It's a game-changer and one of the fastest-growing ways the average individual is creating wealth in this day and age.

The Money Myth

You might be triggered by my masculine words of money and power but we as women need to unapologetically stake equal ownership to these sounds and syllables. Still, it's not about being rich in the traditional sense rather it's about changing the world. You lead best with an audience. Movements are made with active audience members. Just look at Mother Theresa, Martin Luther King Jr., or Princess Diana.

These people were living examples of leaders with followers that made up an audience that continue their legacy until this very day. Money might be able to buy exposure, but it can't buy a loyal audience of action takers. This is the highest level of Audience Currency.

Raving Fans

Fan is short for *fanatic* and having people who are fanatical on your behalf is true wealth that can be leveraged again and again. To maintain raving fans requires responsibility. The best way to earn their allegiance is through your own personal style, approach, attitude, and ideas about life.

Although there is strength in numbers, the truth is that you don't need quantity when many times quality can be just as effective. One die-hard fanatic is worth 1,000 people who only know your name. I've heard and seen men call this their tribe or herd. I'm not sure that's in alignment with my feminine energy. My people are in many ways my chosen family.

After Leaving Home

Even in my early 20s it was the people I met while attending events and conferences that became my people. They were my mentors, my sidekicks and strategic partners. Living on my own, these people became my chosen family members that I liked, loved, and chose to spend time with. This is where I learned to appreciate the sense of community and began to see its value. You are the sum of the people you spend the most time with, so make certain the people around you are the ones you want to be most like.

One person I met early on was Diana Wentworth, who has had her own community of events running for over 30 years. She once explained her approach to audience building as building a playground with all the cool stuff that everyone would want to play on. She is an audience builder with a golden rolodex for sure.

How I Started

I started my community with one simple goal. To give people something they wanted. People wanted exposure, a place to share who they are and what they do. I wanted my audience building to be something beneficial for everyone. It became the *Top Talent* community with events, a magazine, a directory, opportunities to mastermind and even joint venture. It was never about me, rather I just celebrated my people and the successes we were creating together.

I Didn't Have to Sell

As my audience grew and the quality shined, people wanted to be featured, they wanted to speak, they wanted the microphone, they wanted me to introduce them, and promote them - and the more they wanted the more I could ask for in return. Audience Currency attracts attention and opportunities. You go from chasing people to them chasing you and that is wealth.

As my audience wanted more I was strategic about giving it to them through my *Top Talent Magazine, my Top Talent Publishing company, my Top Talent Academy*, and my *Top Talent JV* events. This is a lucrative audience of speakers, authors and experts but more importantly, it's a place that can create positive change in the world. Money has been raised, awareness has been created and new movements are made regularly. This is priceless.

I leveraged my audience to raise money for kids that needed computers, fought human trafficking -and was even a part of celebrities being recruited for this cause, leading to results.

Top Talent Magazine

Being Editor-In-Chief of my own digital magazine has generated several joint venture opportunities because I am able to leverage my positioning and exchange platforms with other show hosts and people of influence so they can get in front of my audience, and in exchange, I can get in front of their people.

Being strategic with this, it follows that with every new edition published, my brand is discussed because of the people spotlighted. My community, whether the members are more recent or have been around longer, sees how we're constantly getting more exposure. When you're able to offer a platform for major players to share their knowledge and insights, it designates you as an authority because of those with whom you are connected. This can be replicated through your own digital magazine, podcasts, shows, Facebook Lives, and any other platform that brings in views.

Bringing In Dylan McDermott

We did a book launch for my client, Je'net Kreitner, at a Gala to raise money for her foundation, *Grandma's House of Hope*. The topic spotlighted the abuse of women and how her foundation was helping the victims of abuse find a 2nd home so they could rebuild their lives, and this caught the attention of actor Dylan McDermott, best known for his role in *The Practice* and *American Horror Story*.

Dylan is a great example of someone who has a massive platform, and, during this Gala, he utilized it to bring awareness and helped my client raise close to $200,000 for her cause. But it also helped that he auctioned himself off for a lunch/dinner special, which I almost won.

When you have reached your ideal audience and have gained the necessary exposure, everything you say and do attracts massive amounts of attention.

When you have a message or belief, that you exemplify multiple times, that is another way to turn fans into loyal followers.

Building A Community

Another word for 'community' that you may have heard of is 'tribe', but both consist of a growing group of people who have the same goals, mission statement, and similar beliefs as you. This allows you to lean on them for support and call on them to band together for a great cause. Over the years, *Top Talent* has developed a community of over 2,600 in our private Facebook group as of March 2022. That may seem small scale for some, but when you need help with a launch, or putting together a group think tank, that number seems pretty outstanding.

To build something like this, the saying goes, "People don't care how much you know until they know how much you care." When you put in true effort into your fans, followers, and believers, then you will continue to develop your community, your tribe.

Sharpening Your Tools

Who you are will change over time with the new people you meet, new experiences, failures, and successes that you have. That means that as you develop, so does your audience. Their belief in you and your goals will either continue to deepen and become stronger or fade away. Those that leave will serve to make room for the new individuals who are just now hearing about you.

Developing your craft so you can hone in on your ideal audience is the tool that you're steadily sharpening over time. This means that when someone new comes into your circle of influence, you have a more powerful positioning because they see the value of it all. They want to have your audience and connect with your people, but in order to do that, you take certain steps to leverage who they are and their audience as well so you can both prosper and grow.

The Name of the Game

It's simple math, really. The more people that hear about what you do, the more likely you are to find the individuals who can afford what you offer. You cannot find success, or at least very much success, by being the world's best-kept secret. To create long-lasting results and see your numbers grow, develop your own platform where people can opt-in, subscribe, like, comment, and share your content. That could be having a show, podcast, event space, digital magazine, or something else on a digital level.

I started to really see everything skyrocket when I started to regularly publish *Top Talent Magazine*. My biggest fans, followers and affiliate partners would have the opportunity to be spotlighted in third party social proof, which they could then share to their database via emails, social media posts, and their websites. In turn, that increased traffic back to the magazine, where I also spotlight everything else I do. Time will need to be invested into a new brand, or an extension of your brand, so when you talk to your people, they can find out new ways that they can get more of you.

These are just a few ways and methods to develop your Audience Currency so you can access these new forms of wealth.

-Isabel Fagan

Isabel Donadio-Fagan is the Founder of Talent Support Services, LLC, DBA Top Talent Agency that includes Top Talent Publishing, Top Talent JV Mastermind Events, Top Talent Membership, Top Talent Speaks, and is Editor-In-Cheif of Top Talent Magazine. She is the best selling author of *Finishing is Happiness: 7 Ways Big Idea Entrepreneurs Can Become Big Business Finishers, Co-Author of Women Gone Wild: The Feminine Guide to Fearless Living and Becoming Significant: How to Invoke Sacred Words That Unlock Real Power*, and the winner of the 2019 TWC Most Outstanding Rising Star Award.

She's regularly featured in the media, including everything from the *Los Angeles Tribune, USA Today, and Forbes.* Her experience includes red-carpet interviewing, magazine publishing, best seller book publishing, and public speaking. Isabel specializes in content creation, authority marketing, and talent management.

May your light shines through all the darkness. You are a beautiful soul ♡
Stefanie

06

YOUR MILLIONAIRE KARMAS

BY STEFANIE BRUNS

"When we combine the idea of prosperity with an intention for our highest good and the highest good of all life, we create true wealth."

- AMY LEIGH MERCREE

When looking at wealth, we must view it from an awareness of the social programming aspect around money, richness, and prosperity. Wealth is a personal journey that is made up of several layers, that start from childhood and early teachings from our parents and teachers. When we go a little deeper, we arrive at the ancestral line and the collective field, and from there we can understand the history of mankind, culture, and the centuries we've viewed the pros and cons of wealth, or the lack thereof.

There are many layers of our early programming, which include the mental aspect and our thought systems, as well as our DNA levels and genomes.

When working with clients, we essentially help with psychological and DNA modifications in order to tap into the multiple layers of the individual. Every person has a special energetic blueprint that is connected to their life experiences, which are complex and differ from person to person. Through testing, we find the root of the problem and release what I call the "millionaire karmas", which are the difficulties or challenges related to their connection to wealth. It is important to release the millionaire karma in order to tap into the field of financial abundance. People that want to go into business, sometimes make the mistake of not practicing a relationship with the energetic and healing aspect of themselves, which can relieve the blockages keeping them caged away from the quantum field.

Energetic Blueprint

Today, as a quantum psychologist, I combine quantum physics, self-development healing, and psychology in the work that I do. Since energy knows no bounds nor borders, we mainly work with our clients online and offer offline services through retreats as well. I am the founder of a marketing company called *Business Flow Academy*, and my focus is on teaching people how to scale their business by going deep into their own energetic blueprint and healing the blockages keeping them stuck.

I identify with being an energy healer, but we are not officially allowed to call it healing, because medicine denies that we have energy systems as humans. Through energy healing, detoxifying the pineal gland, utilizing meditations, and quantum leap hypnosis, we guide people into their ideal state and timeline, where the best version of themself (I call it "Ideal Energetic Signature") lives the life of their dreams. In a state of theta brainwaves, we can easily delete all the old programs and blockages to make space to download all the new skillsets, habits, and knowledge, that their Ideal Energetic Signature already has. Clients describe undergoing massive shifts when we show them how to connect with their intuition and lead them to the direct door of the universal field of their own never-ending wisdom.

Your Life Force

We've developed special healing systems like chakra tapping, neuroenergetic programming, high-frequency healing NFT's and special crystal grids. These methods can help improve people's life force, change their neuroenergetic programming, harmonize their energy system and the environment, lift them up into the abundance frequency or even open intergalactic portals. I want to offer you as a reader of this fabulous book a free downloadable PDF of the Prosperity Grid, which you can print in order to sleep on, meditate with, or put your water onto in order to activate your wealth flow. The grid is also ingrained with gemstone codes, so it is not necessary for people to put their own gemstones on it in order to activate their true potential.

In fact, my connection to my own intergalactic portal has allowed me to develop these unique techniques through information that I download directly from the field of infinite wisdom. This means that I do not learn all my techniques from a physical source, mentor, or schooling - instead, I acquire and create from the information that flows through me to teach and assist others through their healing journey.

I'm originally from Germany, where I worked as a psychologist and business mentor for 10 years until I moved to Portugal.

Story of Belief to Bravery

I will share the story of how I took a chance and changed our situation. It was a rainy, dark and cold autumn afternoon in Germany, about 7 years ago. I was at home with our 2 toddlers and a baby, reflecting on my life and realizing that my husband spent more time with his work colleagues than with us.

I thought *We have studied for so long, two academics, but still we don't have enough money to afford more time together.*

I was a strong entrepreneur who never stopped working, even as a young mother with her children at home and not in daycare. When my husband got home, I started working, when he was on vacation, I held my retreats and workshops. We had 3 wonderful children at this time, two of them born without medical help. The 3rd delivery was more complicated. I was brave enough to have my breech baby at home without the pressures of invasive medicine, but not brave enough to live the life I wanted.

That nasty afternoon, I decided to make a change.

I thought *It must be possible to be in a warmer country during the cold Central European winter months.*

So, 3 months later we sold almost all our stuff and moved to Portugal. I promised my husband that I would cover the costs with my online business, although at the time I had no idea how to do that. We bought a totally overgrown plot of land and lived in a yurt for 1 year. We built a permaculture garden, a small house out of a ruin.

Not So Romantic

All of this would sound super romantic, but we had a big problem: My online business started well, but I couldn't scale it. After 6 months we were left with no money or savings, no relatives or friends who could help. There was great suffering at this time, and we nearly resorted to selling our wedding rings in order to afford groceries. This was and emotional decision but due to the low offer, we kept them. The summer was full of fear but eventually, it was autumn and we went to Germany where I had a speaker performance. When I looked at my phone the next day, people texted me, "Are you still alive?" There had been a "huge forest fire" right on our property.

Everything was gone, but my first thought was *Okay, the fire can take our goods, the acre of forest, our garden, but it cannot burn my knowledge.*

Three months later after we cut down all the burned trees we went to the beach. I had all my online office equipment with me because that's all I had to make money. When we came back, we saw that a thief had stolen all my last resources!

But here, too, my first thought was *Nobody can steal my knowledge.*

Three years later, there was an abrupt falling out with my former business partner. Again, my first thought was: *Nobody can steal my knowledge, my creativity, my unstoppable faith.*

I developed my own business concept within 24 hours, and that was 20 months ago. I started my online business from scratch and taught myself how to create videos, and how set up programs. I worked 80-90 hours a week, but I grew it into a multi-million-dollar business.

Energy Field

The only possibility of a bright future for my family and myself in Portugal was my connection to the energy field. When you have a connection to the field and the infinite wisdom of all that is, you know exactly what to do without a shadow of a doubt. Within a short amount of time, I was generating six figures a month and had set up a multi-million-dollar business with my special approach to wealth creation, which I am teaching now to my clients.

The reason I'm sharing this with you: There's no excuse! If a simple girl from central Germany can do it, you can too. No fire, no thief, no treachery can stop you. There is literally nothing stopping you from improving your game.

Revolutionized

I've been doing this kind of work for over 17 years and have noticed quite an evolution in people becoming more open to inner work and healing today. It is much more spoken about and has inspired an awakened community to explore their extrasensory perceptions. We always hear about "The Great Awakening", a phase hopefully within the near future where we see all people in the world revolutionized by their inner wisdom, however, compared to 20 years ago, I see that we have evolved closer to that phase at a fantastic rate.

Everybody is connected to the quantum field and when you find the link you come into connection with your own inner peace, joy, and love. Most people in business that have found the link to the field are usually spiritually connected but have yet to connect themselves to physical wealth gain; these are usually the blockages we must work to relieve in order to receive our endless streams of abundance.

The Birthright

Prosperity is our birthright, and many people that come to me struggle with imposter syndrome or tend to think that they are undeserving of their intrinsic wealth. When we release those blockages, we can enter a new world of the intergalactic portals within ourselves where we house our wealth. As human beings, it is within our reach to be in spiritual and monetary alignment.

Additionally, as infinite beings, I don't believe we have limitations. There is no reason to choose between being more spiritual or more business-oriented. We have the ability and resources to heal and embody our cosmic mission that brings us both.

The best way people can be aligned to their cosmic mission starts with identifying what that is. What does fulfilling your mission in this life feel like on your body? What emotions does it bring out of you? When we are not aligned to our cosmic mission, we find ourselves feeling unfulfilled or unhappy. The most important thing to remember is that our goal setting and vision must be aligned with our cosmic mission. Through special hypnosis, I help people uncover their cosmic mission by going through their ideal timelines as if they have already achieved it.

Internal Feedback

They describe the feelings they feel, which are connected to their internal feedback system. Everybody has a feedback system that is sharpened through healing work. When people go about their day-to-day, they can better sense when they are getting closer and warmer to what excites and energizes the extrasensory systems of their ideal timeline.

I like to believe that our extrasensory perception, this so-called sixth sense, is actually just our normal perception that consists of blockages that need to be healed. When we find our cosmic mission, it is an undeniable feeling. The universe starts talking to you all the time, and if you find yourself dealing with doubt, you can always ask for signs from the universe that will define things more precisely.

Juiciness of Life

The proof that our systems are successfully working is not only the outstanding results of my clients but also, I had to restart my company two years ago after my former business partners and I went in separate directions; I created my business into an empire. The suffering phase is what I view as the boot camp of my life. All the challenges that presented themselves at the time seemed so illogical, but eventually made complete sense, when I realize how much they forced me to step into my power. We see that some of the most successful individuals are those who undergo much grief before they can experience the juiciness of life. When something big and sometimes sudden happens in our lives, it is the test of time and is simply there to create us into the leaders of our journey.

Cosmic Orgasm

Life is not about earning millions and wealth is not an unforeseeable concept. To me, wealth in our lives is about the reward of doing something meaningful and creating change in the life of others. We all have a unique journey that comes down to finding and aligning with the wealth that sits silently hidden within ourselves. When we awaken our energy systems we can then embark on our rightful path.

I call it a "cosmic orgasm" because there's no feeling like that of fulfilling your cosmic mission and experiencing it in its totality.

-Stefanie Bruns

Stefanie Bruns helps extraordinary world leaders achieve outstanding results and experiences. She is an expert in leading high performers to more life force, energy, and success.

Stefanie is a quantum psychologist, business mentor, and mother of 4 children with over 20 years of experience coaching ultra-successful people using methods that others would call crazy and spiritual - but that's the sparkle of the omniverse that we are here to discover. Her teachings, healings, and mentoring are like magical antidotes from the womb of the galaxy.

Stefanie Bruns is renowned for creating rapid shifts within the energetic fields of her clients and their business that lead to healing, enhancements and a massive increase in vibrancy.

Her work is internationally appreciated in *Forbes, Influencive, Disrupt, The Entrepreneur Magazine, Daily Star, Hollywood Digest,* and more.

MELISSA —

YOU ARE SO MUCH
BIGGER THAN YOU THINK
YOU ARE!

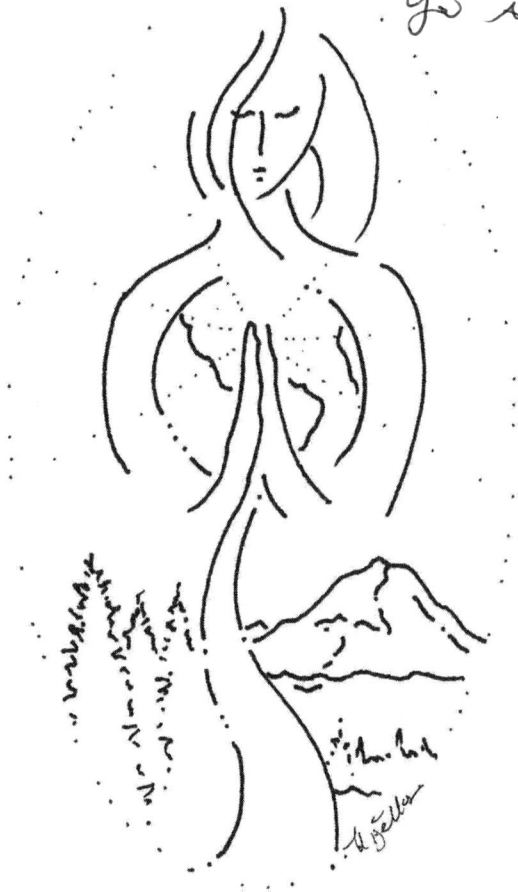

♥ CAMBERLY

07

SILENCE IS GOLDEN

BY CAMBERLY GILMARTIN

"The life of consciousness and energy supporting the stars and galaxies is also supporting us; for we are participants of this Eternal Mystery."

- JOSEPH CAMPBELL

I'm slow. After years of resistance, I have gratefully discovered the immense value of slowing down, and of stillness. I've adopted the realization that this 'slower' way of being, close observation of, and connection to nature and animals has positively influenced my perspectives and distinctly shaped my experiences and beliefs. It is said that health is wealth. For me, the root of health lies in the ability to connect to our stillness within; to quiet the rush of continual thinking, and unite with our own calm, steady heart.

A Force Greater than Myself

I've heard it said that we are each born connected to our hearts, then grow up, and spend the rest of our lives figuring out how to reconnect with that place within ourselves! I consider myself fortunate to have remained connected to my heart space during my lifetime. I believe that this was possible because, as a child, I learned to operate from a place of feeling which I experienced most strongly while in nature. Especially in forests, at the tops of high mountains, and near water, I sensed the presence of and felt deeply connected with a force much greater than myself. There, a flow of information, questions, and answers continually sprung forth and I intuitively trusted these.

It wasn't until years later that I came to understand at a conscious level that what I was experiencing was a connection with my heart space – soul – power – divine essence – spirit – I invite you to go ahead and imagine whatever name you may use to refer to this concept for yourself here. When connected to my heart space, I also understood all at once that my life force was deeply connected to every single atom, every human, plant, animal, and inanimate object. Later, I began to fully understand that it was possible to tap into this vast stillness to seek answers, ask for aid, serve humanity, and create abundance in my life.

Soft Spoken Tomboy

During the summer before I was to start high school, my parents moved us from a small town in Minnesota to the Pacific Northwest. Life was faster on the West Coast! It was a tough adjustment for a soft-spoken tomboy who rode her 10-speed to school and spent more time inside books than studying fashion or make-up, however, eventually I managed to find my place. Thankfully, the shimmering Emerald City of Seattle offered plenty of nature; water, trees, and mountains allowing me to continually connect with both beauty and abundance – though I had yet to use the term abundance consciously.

During high school, I honed my love for writing, and the practice of yoga and meditation entered my life. Immediately, the yogic teachings felt like old friends, and the knowledge and regular practice of yoga and meditation was a tremendous relief during the turbulent teen years when I, like many young people, was seeking to understand my true self. I would often escape the feelings of uncertainty about where I fit into life by heading to the mountains to ski or hike, or the lake to row or sail. I enjoyed sports, animals, and being active. I also paid close attention to what I ate to maintain a physically strong body and mind.

Nature has always been a safe haven for me. To be able to hear, feel, and connect with the stillness of my heart space, I intuitively knew that I needed to be silent in and with nature. At the same time, experiencing this connection allowed me to both feel and understand at a very deep level that I was enough – that I did not need anything else to feel the highest high, and deepest love imaginable. And this truth exists for every single one of us everywhere when we learn how to tap into it!

The Secret to True Abundance

This is a crucial message for humanity right now, and especially for our children and teens as addiction, homelessness, mental health crises, violence, sex crimes, suicide, and the list of illnesses caused by disconnection to our heart spaces, and one another grows longer.

When was the last time you sat silently in the beauty of nature and allowed your heart to be filled with its abundance? This abundance also exists within you. We are all one. There is no separation. Where one is suffering pain and sorrow, the whole suffers. The reverse is also true. Where one is experiencing deep joy and love, the entire universe benefits.

The thing I want to be sure that every reader understands is that learning to connect to and move from the stillness in your heart isn't especially complicated, and yet it's not so simple either. It requires unplugging ourselves from what we have been taught. We must cease listening to our guts - and instead, tune into what our hearts are saying. As soon as our mind, or gut, becomes involved, ego arrives. The ego can often steer us astray, whereas the heart can never be wrong.

Learning to Listen

Learning to listen to the heart takes patience and courage because the answers are not always shown at once. Often struggle, hardship and pain get in the way of the truth we seek. In my life experience, I have learned that this is not necessary. Struggle and pain may help us become resilient, believe, and know that we are strong - yet these are actually ego and disconnect us from the stillness within. In my life, I have experienced my fair share of heartbreak, pain, and sadness. One of the biggest was a divorce from the father of my children, whom I loved very deeply.

Through these experiences, I have learned that I have the choice to immediately connect into my heart space instead of into ego and pain. This is an incredibly powerful insight.

I often explain the insight I gained from my divorce as the tearing up of my Norman Rockwell painting. You likely can imagine the scene – a perfectly coiffed couple around an immaculately set table with smiling, well-dressed children, an obedient dog at their side – and let's not forget a white picket fence! I needed to mourn this ideal vision as I set out on my journey as a divorced, single mom.

The Feeling Frequency

Ultimately the valuable message I gained is that life is not a straight line. It's a beautiful, crooked one. And that's okay. You are exactly where you are meant to be right now. In this world, there are many, many different lines for you to choose from. What is important is how you are feeling and what you are learning on the journey. Tapping into the stillness within your heart allows you to understand this. There is a myriad of other voices around us and it can be difficult to discern our own. You need only to listen to your voice though, because that very voice is your heart, and the heart is never wrong. Every hardship and difficult turn are meant to inform, teach, help you to listen even more closely, and then refine. This work takes patience, courage, and a willingness to spend time in silence and nature – and is SO worth it!

Over the last five years, I have gotten a divorce, worked a full-time job, started a company, sold my house, moved my two children and myself in with my aging parents, started and finished an MBA program, assisted my eighty-nine-year-old friend in the completion of her memoir, and helped to launch a community non-profit – while (at times turbulently) raising two teens during a global pandemic. There were many days when I wondered how I would manage to survive the hour, much less the week. I tell you this because I want everyone reading this who may be doubting themself to understand that if I could do all this (and more) then so can you! The beautiful thing is, it all becomes easier when you are connected to and moving from the stillness within your heart! Abundance is awaiting your arrival in your heart.

As I continue to intentionally connect with and live from the stillness within my heart, I have started to notice that there is an inner knowingness that informs me about every project I involve myself in or agree to work on. Within the last two years, it's become clear that all things I am working on make sense and are connected. They have all led me to the very message I am imparting here: We are all one. Abundance exists everywhere.

Doing Your Divine

Six years ago, through an unlikely introduction, I met Victoria Chassé and began working with her on her book, *Tasting the Essence of One's Godly Self.* The entire subject of Victoria's book is connecting to your divine self. Four years ago, thanks to my divorce I ended up taking a new job into which Nancy Gellos walked one day. We talked for two hours and knew we were destined to work together. This knowingness manifested into working with her and Maybin Chisebuka on tBUG, a global community garden space with a shared dream of universal importance: that the food we eat is inseparable from the land and conditions in which it is grown. Healthy food is the root of healthy kids, families, community, wellness, and connection. And here I am today co-authoring this amazing book. As a result, I've also co-authored a chapter in another collaborative book project. These projects are all about tapping into Abundance. None of this is happening by accident. We are all deeply connected.

How to be Enough

My desire for each of you reading this is that you will intentionally take some time to slow down, hear, and connect with the stillness within your heart so that you may see that you, exactly as you are, are enough. Once we comprehend this then fear, stress, and unhappiness can no longer be sustained within us more than briefly. There is only unescapable joy, deep peace, and gratitude. All at once the entire universe and all things embrace us in a connected love. Stillness in and of itself is something that must be prioritized and those people that do, find themselves in a state of true abundance. This defines wealth to me. Imagine a world in which each of us firmly believes we are enough and are connected to our hearts. Imagine the domino effect this would have. What a breathtakingly beautiful thought this is.

-Camberly Gilmartin

Camberly Gilmartin is an entrepreneur, businesswoman, author, parent, and active change advocate for businesses, people, and the planet. She has learned that action is the catalyst for creating positive change and believes that the world is ready for a shift at a significant level. Her passion is to inspire others to connect with their hearts, create a life of health, joy, abundance, and peace, and raise their vibration - so that they may inspire others around them to do the same.

Melisa

May your soul
keep shining

love
xx

08

FEARLESS LIVING

BY KAREN WHELAN

"We want you to spend vibrational currency, not money."

- ABRAHAM HICKS

Living in creation is fearless living. How many of us can say we have walked the terrain of our inner abyss and found our way home - home to the truth of ourselves.

The way out IS the way in. I say this and believe it truly because it applies to all that we endure. You can also apply this phrase when it comes to wealth because to not know your spiritual being is to be in debt to life and the systems that are set up against your authentic self. When you're not living your authentic self, that is pure deprivation. Life, according to my spiritual teacher "is not meant to hurt you, it's meant to wake you up to the truth of who you are."

My Mother's Fear

I was born into a family with a lot of fear and programming. We grew up in fear of money, never having enough. A memory that embedded itself deep in my being was being 6-years old when my parents had to hide us one day under the bed because our landlord was knocking on our door looking for the rent. I remember witnessing my mother's fear, and that's when I realized that my safety and my world are very sensitive, and anything can change in a heartbeat. Lack filtered into my world on this day and like an uncompliant guest, it never left till I became 37.

A Shrinking World

Your fears, like mine, disconnected me in a big way. I was abused growing up. As I got older, I began to self-hate – my trust and love in myself and the world had shrunk. As you know self-hate leads us down a path of self-sabotage, where I began hating my physical form and attempted to take my life at 15. I was disconnected from myself, and in essence, I was disconnected from Source!

> "We all come from a source that you can call God, divine, doesn't matter what we call it. And this source is everywhere there is no place that it is not it must be because it creates everything; everything comes from this source. Then it must be in me if there is no place that it is not in then it must be in me."
>
> - DR. WAYNE DYER.

When you know it, this is when you are born out of humanity and into divinity!

Disconnecting from Source saw me doubt Karen and turn my back on myself and project that life was threatening, and this saw me having a *lack filter* in which I saw absence and impossibility in everything!

Your life shouldn't be around maintaining the status quo. Where you are trying to make it in the world, compete against everyone else just to be and feel like somebody. So, it's all about ambition but with no purpose. Can you identify with this? This is how it was for me when I never felt worthy or good enough. I looked at Karen with lack and believed I needed to be something in order to be accepted.

I would compare my body to other women and always find something wrong with myself. At that point in my life, due to my cynical outlook, I had no sense of anything spiritual and numbed my true depth by not caring about anything, only what others thought of me. I lived on the edge for a couple of years with drugs until I chose to leave home at 17 to work as an au pair for an incredible woman who was a healer in France. She taught me about the power of forgiveness and how holding onto hate will manifest as illness in the body.

Compassion for Your Own Humanity

For me, I decided to reframe the story and see that the soul was meant for the journey it endured. That is what I teach my clients today; to hold forgiveness and compassion for their humanity. This informs my work as a psychotherapist, tantric teacher, and energy healer. In other words, I do short-term transformational therapy and take interest in helping people connect to their authentic selves. I work with teens and adults and offer sessions, workshops, and retreats. I am a soul whisperer where your soul tells me what's going on. Our souls co-create the pathway home.

I used to dismiss that power I had because conventional therapy training doesn't allow for that. I had to shut that side down when I was learning how to be a therapist. Now I realize that your body can be so attuned to the other person that you can hear what the soul needs. What's blocking their growth? And what do you need to see your light?

Crying, Not Eating

When I was 37, my 14-year relationship came to an end, and I had to declare myself homeless with my two grown kids. It was a challenging time and for me was a shameful moment. A period of spiritual desolation. Here I was a 37-year-old psychotherapist, appearing to be falling apart from the outside, but on the inside, I was deconstructing and starting to realize my true self.

I spent eight intense days of crying, not eating, not sleeping, and reflecting on all the things I had done in my life that made me the person I was. I was doing everything for everybody else and would abandon myself to people-please. I did it to be liked, because I had rejected myself so much, and learned to put more value on what people thought of me. My inner frame of reference was: it matters what I think you think of me!

I was stripped so bare during those eight days and nights. I was physically cocooning and internally transforming. I was having intense and vivid dreams. It was eight days of enlightened downloads and purging the notions of what it meant to be me.

One of the nights, I went to bed and had a dream that I was in a consciousness space-traveling alongside the divine. I heard a voice communicating with me, not dialectally, but like a thought. It asked, "Do you know what you're coming in for?" and when I said, "Yes," I was inside my mother's womb, hearing the heartbeat, overwhelmed by the sensation of losing the knowing of my divine self.

I was told in the dream that everything holds a program - the food you eat, so are you making it with joy or negativity? As this is the vibration you will consume. Your mind is such a fertile ground and is influenced daily by what you watch or read. The truth was to go beyond the programs and find myself which could only be done in meditation.

Hence, the way out is the way in.

I then booked my three-day silence retreat with the Benedictine monks. I began detaching from the version and identity of my old self. It was complete internal death and on day eight, it was something like an ascension when I heard a voice inside of me say, "Come home, it's time to come home to yourself."

Holding Trauma

When I immersed myself further into meditation and unraveling my truth, I was in a lot of pain and physically couldn't move from my bed for 11 days. My body had held a lot of trauma and it was being triggered by the amount of healing work I was doing to expel it. One of the nights, I had a vivid vision and was visited by a celestial goddess at the end of my bed, in gorgeous clothes, who was holding my inner child who was holding a red rose. When I saw her, I knew her, she was a part of me. My inner child then handed me the red rose and the minute I reached for the red rose, my physical pain was gone. I looked up the meaning of a red rose and found that it symbolizes the end of trauma. I couldn't believe it; I was able to lift myself from the burden of the pain and the hate from my adolescence.

Being the Butterfly

After a lifetime of trauma, my metamorphosising moment came like a cocooned caterpillar emerging as a beautiful butterfly. When you take a closer look, you can see that the caterpillar has no idea that it's destined to be a butterfly, but the intelligent cells know. The behaviour of the caterpillar changes and it cocoons itself in preparation to become the butterfly. I had the intelligence and resonance of that caterpillar and essentially knew what had to be done energetically. This is alchemy at its most divine.

The fear of "not making it" completely left my perspective. This inner shift allowed me to be and feel liberated from living indebted to society as I no longer strived for ambition and to fit in. I was now living from purpose and meaning.

I stopped being afraid of price tags and rejected the emphasis on possessing things. NO-thing out there can give me what the ME within can! Can you trust this aspect of yourself? Can you sit in space yet feel deeply embraced by the essence of your own presence? Can you breathe into a knowing that all that truly matters is the mystery, magic, and richness that lies within all of us? When you have that, everything else aligns on an energetic level. When everything was stripped away from me, I found myself and was left with this one truth. I had unbecome all that I had become and knew by being born I was accepting my inheritance from the Divine.

Stuck Fake

I retired back to a childlike place where I believed in magic, tapping into simplicity, and treating life like a wonderful playground. When we armour up, we forget who we are and lose the connection to the divine. I was so stuck in this fake version of myself until life put so much pressure on me to deconstruct and disarm allowing me to melt back into God and see through the eyes of innocence. My relationship with the divine now became my priority.

Richness is being able to taste the essence of your presence and celebrate the mystery and wonderment of being alive inside of yourself - that to me is what wealth is all about. I had physical wealth then, and as part of the divine plan, I lost it all because energetically I was not ready to hold it. You can have money in the bank and be broken inside, with little or no happiness or inner peace. This happens because the way to inner peace is when you are happy and accept the truth about who you are, and to know it and live it is enriching. Tasting the essence of your presence is embodying the wisdom of knowing you are worthy; "I AM Worthy". To truly know "I AM Worthy" is you attuning to the infinite power of your enlightened self.

God in Me as Me in God

To be truly able to feel, say and know I am worthy is awakened to the mind in you that knows the words I AM is Christ Consciousness; a knowing of God in you. Who works in you, through you, and as you, and the words you add to the I Am-ness becomes the soul's expression of consciousness and this is an unstoppable force.

Worth has always been understood as an external validation received based on the material and financial attainments in your life. However, if these are lost then that worth attached to them also goes. The worth I'm speaking of and pointing to is the divine self within that does not go away or grow because of physical wealth- you do not lose your true inner source when you lose money or material objects.

We all individually have an incredible blueprint. You are destined to become this God spark. The breakdown that I had was a perfect representation of the Divine Will. Maybe on some level, we are all here to witness that divinity. I saw it as a miracle opportunity. It was a poetic justice done unto the soul because the soul asked for it – it was waiting and looking for that transformation. I saw that there's nothing to fear because it's an ascension to profound wisdom. It's a gift (pre-sent).

Our souls always know where we are going and we're not meant to turn our back on our light. If my job is to remind people of that, then I am blessed.

True Wealth

So why am I sharing my personal story with you and not speaking of financial wealth? In truth, what we are all looking for is the source within the blueprint that we are destined to be. We are all spiritual beings having a human experience. When born we take on so many programs and lose that ability to truly see ourselves. Sometimes we get glimpses of it in a beautiful connection with someone and we share ourselves in a real way. There is such profoundness to that, and that profoundness is invaluable. That profoundness is the heart's wisdom, the heart knowing of itself. That is invaluable and when you have that there is a satisfaction that is always awakened inside of you. You are tasting the essence of your presence, the gold of your soul. Suddenly, the things out there begin to look like just things. So, what happens then is wherever you go no matter what it is that you are doing, you will feel so rich, you will experience a true richness in every unfolding moment. This is a hidden treasure that is worth finding.

-Karen Whelan

Karen Whelan is a Transformational Psychotherapist, intuitive consultant, Tantric teacher, Rising Star Healer, workshop facilitator, retreat leader & author of 2 memoirs. Karen is also the founder of *Soulution Therapy* offering transformative services to Companies, individuals, groups, couples, and teenagers. Karen has worked with clients for over 14 years and witnessed thousands of clients transform their lives. Her work has brought her to sit with world experts such as Dr. Joe Dispenza, and with Gabor Mate training in Living Inquiries, as well as the incredible spiritual teacher - humanitarian & wellness expert, Derek O'Neil. Her work has seen Karen on TV, Radio, writing for a monthly column offering wellness tips, being a keynote speaker on the *Women Gone Wild Summit 2021*, and being featured in *Los Angeles Weekly Times, Hollywood Digest, Yahoo News, Thrive Global*, and more.

With love +
love +
positive energy
always [signature]

09

FAILURE LEADS TO SUCCESS

BY KORTNEY MURRAY

"I do not think I am successful just because I have money. I'm successful because I love who I am and I have no regrets."

– SUZE ORMAN

This is a story about "KAOS" to "KAPITAL" and it starts with Kortney with a "K". I grew up with a supportive family that believed in the traditional styles of raising their children; good education leads to a good-paying job with benefits, you know, the "American way". What my mom and dad don't know is that they taught me so much more than that within my upbringing. My mother stayed home to raise my brother and me and supported all our activities - from sports to schooling and everything in between. My father climbed the ladder of entrepreneurship and all the while, a dedicated father.

My parents were never scared to teach us hard work ethic due to their own upbringing; like my mother being one of six children with a father that worked in the factory, and my father being raised by his grandmother who was an immigrant from Lebanon.

Working hard to make something of myself was simply in my blood, but being a woman from a highly dominant, patriotic family was always what drove me to succeed. I wanted to show the world from a young age that I could do anything I set my mind to. I did not allow myself to sit inside a box of limitations, so I packed my car and headed to college to experience the rocky waters of becoming an independent woman on my own.

Rhino Walking

When I got to college, I was thrilled to discover my tribe. After 27 years of friendship, I can look back and say those four women helped mold me into who I am today. The past five years have been something I like to call "tragic beauty". We have a motto in our group: "Walk like a beautiful rhino, with thick skin and never looking backward." To us, this means not letting the hardships of our past define us, but instead using them to create better futures. I am now 46, and from the time I was 40 we have experienced some major losses in the friend group: one lost their husband, one lost a child, I lost my father, and one passed away after fighting hard against breast cancer. Our meeting venues changed from annual girls' trips to funerals.

These experiences were not easy to get through, and I still battle them every day, but I'm grateful for the lessons

I've learned. The world became a much smaller place, and my desire to share empathy and compassion with others grew stronger. My success has been formed on the foundation of pain, loss, experience, and downright hard work. The failures I had led to my success and the grace it takes to create a business that offers a partnership to our clients.

After going through tough relationships and my all-too-relatable early twenties after college, I decided to redirect my focus back to becoming the best version of myself. I chose to truly love and learn about myself. I gained more self-confidence and dove into becoming a successful woman. I got yoga certified alongside my husband, Chris, which had always been a goal of mine. It helped with my mental clarity and stability, and it shows in the way I operate my business today.

Not Optional

Mental health is important and making time for oneself is not something I believe should be treated as an option. For a woman to thrive in a man's world, it is vital to still *feel* like a woman: beautiful yet strong, feminine but with a voice, teacher but always a student.

My first position after college was selling cars, which was my ticket out of Michigan. I moved to Atlanta to start my life, my own identity and my desire to succeed were greater than ever. I found out quickly I had a knack for sales, so much so that while selling a car, I was offered a dream of a career working for Creative Loafing in Atlanta, GA. I realized that each sales career was a steppingstone in the "ABI" method (Always Be Interviewing).

One job turned into another until I landed one that took me all the way to California.

"Left my home in Georgia and headed for the Frisco Bay"

- OTIS REDDING

The position I was offered was not so glamorous, but it sure did teach me to have perseverance and strength. It was a commission-based, extremely high turnover door-to-door sales position. It didn't take long for my friends and family to question what type of seemingly cult-like structure I was drinking the Kool-Aid from. The position gave me the tools necessary to teach myself and my current staff today the law of averages, fear of loss, a sense of urgency, and a good, honest, hard work ethic.

Gypsy Free

San Francisco eventually got old for this gypsy, so I took a position selling heavy equipment and moved to San Diego with a few miscellaneous jobs in between. In time, this led me to step into an opportunity that forever changed my life: KAOS was born. One day, I walked into a clothing store called the CooCoo Caterpillar in Cardiff by the Sea. The owner at the time was 8 months pregnant and overheating from the brutal California heat. She saw me and quickly asked if I wanted to buy her store. Fashion and I went hand-in-hand; even without a dime to my name, I had to have nice shoes. I took the leap.

What a freeing feeling! I may not have known how to operate the cash register, but I knew how to make people look and feel beautiful. I rounded up my friends and family and started making the store my own. I didn't have a clue where to get clothes to sell, so I started upselling TJ Maxx products until I found my way. I found the name KAOS to be fitting as I am Kortney with a 'K' and it was my first step onto the rocky boat of the open sea.

Crumbling Clothing Store

Ultimately, the boutique crumbled. It was not from lack of heart or sweat equity, rather, it failed because I was uneducated when it came to finances.

The failure led me to realize that small business owners face enormous financial challenges, many of which are often hidden from them until it's too late.

After losing KAOS, I ended up working as an account executive for equipment financing and working capital for business-to-business. Through the process of opening and losing KAOS, I desired to reach a better understanding of what it meant to co-mingle your personal funds with your business funds. I also wanted to present the newfound knowledge to other women entrepreneurs so they wouldn't fail due to finances. I promptly learned about the other arm of the banking institutions, business, and smart financing.

My Way

As my knowledge of the industry grew, so did my passion for serving up superior customer service and relationship lending. I knew I wanted to do things my way which inevitably led me to jump ship to form my own company in 2007, *Farhat Leasing, LLC* - the springboard to what is known today as *Coastal Kapital, LLC.*

Now, more than one person has called coastal kapital a dream maker. As one of the leading financial firms in Florida, I have taken *Coastal Kapital* to new heights and achieved accreditation for the company as a direct lender. This achievement, coupled with the fact that I meticulously documented my successes (and failures), and developed a proven process for leveraging financial tools, affords *Coastal Kapital* the unique ability to deliver a 360° financial partner experience.

Coastal Kapital offers women a consultative approach to expanding their empires with avenues and aggressive programs for financing, lines of credit, SBA loans, and all-around consulting on their business needs and growth.

Growing with Friends

In our recent years of growth, I chose to create a culture in our staff that welcomes laughter and close relationships, accompanied by the expectation that they are working hard and creating new opportunities consistently. Something I learned over time is how important it is to be a mentor to other women, including the friends you keep. My company is currently made up of my husband of 12 years and a few of my long-term friends like my middle school buddy, Erin NesSmith, my first college roommate, and long-time friend, Heather Panzitta, who is now *Coastal Kapital's* Head of Funding, along with many others that make up our office family.

It is incredibly rewarding to sit back and see how far we've all come. Working side-by-side and supporting each other in all our successes is such a blessing.

My work is truly fantastic, but one of the outcomes that I hold close to my heart is being married to my best friend and true love, Christopher Murray, for 12 years and counting. We currently reside in Sarasota, Florida, actively growing *Coastal Kapital* and assisting businesses all over the country. Our little family consists of our four furry rescue felines, who hold down the fort on the days we enjoy the open water on our boat or head out of town for a quick adventure!

-Kortney Murray

Oozing with optimism, Kortney Murray is one of the most connected female business leaders on the East Coast in an arena saturated with men. At 22, Kortney opened her first business–that ultimately crumbled–but not from lack of heart; but rather her own inexperience when it came to financing. Failure led her to realize that business owners face enormous financial challenges, many of which are often hidden from them until it's too late. Today, Kortney heads up *Coastal Kapital*, her self-made, financial services company in Florida, whose mission is to guide others through the choppy waters of business financing.

10

FREEDOM TO CHOOSE

BY SHAR MOORE

"Wealth is the ability to fully experience life."

- HENRY DAVID THOREAU

When we think of wealth, most people think about the monetary side. While that is a fact, I believe that freedom of choice is the most important thing to look at when defining wealth. Money allows us the freedom to choose our jobs, relationships, having kids, and the foods we consume - all of which gives a sense of the wealth in our lives.

I was born in Thailand then I moved to Australia at the age of 4, and by the time I was 11, it was organized by the hierarchy of my family and traditional Indian culture, to engage me with a man who was 9 years older than me. My Australian stepdad who had raised me well, found out about this tradition when I was 15 and asked if this was something that I wanted to do. Nobody made me feel that I had a choice because I was simply told that this was part of the culture. I had seen it so much growing up in Thailand where young girls were getting married all the time and thought it was normal. It was then when my stepdad had asked me that I realized it wasn't all that normal after all. He reminded me that as an Australian citizen I had the option to say no – to which I did. I didn't know it at the time, but it was a very important decision when I fully realized that I wanted to go to school, get a job, and meet someone naturally later. It was a pivotal moment in my life that I carry with me today because it shaped my belief that when one person believes in you, anything is possible. Here I was, 6 months from being married and moving to a different country away from everything I knew, and by a stroke of some miracle, I was presented with a path that I could claim as my own.

I had the freedom to choose. I had wealth.

After a long journey at the age of 17, I moved out and started working right away. I met my husband at my first job and had our first son when I was 22. Today we have two boys who are 28 and 24 and our daughter is 18. We traveled the world and lived overseas in Thailand and Dubai where I took on many corporate jobs in the spa and hotel industry.

Wealth of Ambition

These big decisions around wealth came to me when I had no formal experience, hardly finished high school, didn't get a college degree, but had an overflowing amount of ambition. I recall some of the wealthiest moments in my life were those like when I was sitting at an interview within a beautiful new 5-star hotel in Bangkok, and the general manager told me how he sees my potential, despite my background and where I come from. It was one of those pivotal moments where I felt seen, and all it took was a believer to unfold the possibility of anything. I became the hotel's executive assistant which moved me forward to future opportunities in corporate positions with other companies in Thailand and led me to eventually open my day spa in the Middle East.

When we decided to move back to Australia, I opened a fashion boutique and worked as a personal stylist. It was an amazing career and I helped women transform into their upgraded style while encouraging them to feel good in new colors and clothing that suited their personalities. Unfortunately, it was a rather short-lived career as we were indirectly affected by the Queensland floods in 2011. One minute I'm running a thriving business, and the next I'm facing bankruptcy. The whole event brought back a lot of old limiting beliefs I had about myself growing up. They stemmed from the times that I would always hear that I was "just an Indian girl", and that I should remain quiet until I fulfilled my role as a man's wife one day. The voices were loud and turned into an internal crescendo saying, "They were right, you shouldn't have started a business."

Shifted Paths

As mentioned, there are many key moments in my journey that have made me feel the wealthiest in my life. My experience is full of ups and downs, and I knew the possibility of another up wasn't far from reach. I wanted to find a way to express women's empowerment through a magazine that wasn't centered around celebrities or gossip, but one directed toward real, everyday women regarding business, life stories, experiences that women have undergone, and how they shifted their paths. When I scanned the local newsstands, I couldn't find a magazine close to the concept - so I started one myself.

I've always been interested in women's empowerment. Due to the circumstances that I have been through, it is in my nature to help other women be their best versions. Nurturing women is truly engrained in everything that I do.

Empowered Publishing

Though I didn't have any experience in the publishing industry, I felt very empowered by the decision in creating YMAG.com.au. The concept of the magazine was around women's why, and profiling women in business based on why they got out of bed every day. We ran the digital magazine for close to 5 years until our readers crowdfunded us to get their hands on physical copies as well. It was an amazing and collaborative moment to be taken from digital to print and running the magazine for a total of 9 years. We eventually moved on to publishing our current magazine called Feminessence, which is geared toward women to tap into their feminine essence and powerful innate abilities. We publish magazines, anthology books, and host retreats through our brand, through my publishing company Sharanis Publishing House on the Gold Coast, Australia.

Brought Home

One of my favorite key moments through this journey of life and creating my business is when I had the incredible opportunity to share my story on a TedX stage. I always thought that the TedX stage was exclusively for the people that had made it, and when I was invited to share my story it inarguably brought everything home.

I can honestly say that I accidentally fell into the publishing industry which turned into my biggest business achievement. I was going bankrupt, but I had just enough money to buy a magazine off a shelf, with a vision to change the entire landscape for women. I had no funds nor the knowledge or know-how.

I just knew it was something that was happening from a fiercely honest place. It wasn't just a frivolous business decision, because I felt it from a deep place within my core. I was told that I was crazy by my peers to even attempt launching print magazines since a lot of bigger magazine names were going full digital. I barely even had the means to launch a digital magazine, but when we did, the success progressed into crowdfunding of over $20,000 to print and expand. We went the opposite direction and against the grain of conventional magazine launching which became part of our success. Another part was in muting the repetitive lull of celebrities, diets, fashion, and messages that could negatively affect women, and instead replacing it all with real people and knowledge that could elevate the lives of our readers. I've been in business for 17 years now, and I continue to generate ideas that propel our message to the world.

Banter Beautiful

I'm very excited for women to look out for our upcoming live TV talk show, with a live audience of a couple of hundred people, called The Girlfriend Hour TV airing mid-year. The show will have a nice flow of banter between our guests where they will share their stories by holding space for women to proudly share their wins and challenges. It's that beautiful flow and energy that women have when they get together and know that they are in a safe space to share anything. Women have been silenced and suppressed for so long and the show is about women controlling the narrative. I truly believe we can lift the positivity and vibration of humanity when we join together in this way.

Oxygen of Believers

We all have an inner GPS, also known as our intuition, that is always communicating with us. The way to hear if we are going in the correct direction in life is through focusing our hearing on our GPS systems. By spending time with our thoughts, we can take from our initial thoughts as truths. Though we may dismiss them at first, they will eventually need to be explored, because that is how we are unearthing our truest wealth. I also believe in the power of community, because when you share the oxygen of people who believe in you, the more you can breathe the same to yourself.

To quote from one of my favorite movies, *We Bought a Zoo* - "It just takes 20 seconds of insane courage."

-Shar Moore

Shar Moore is recognized as a TV talk show host, multi-international award-winning mentor, international best-selling author, keynote speaker, and founder of the *Feminessence®️ Movement*. She appears regularly in the media, with features on Studio 10 TV, 7 News, 9 News, MSN U.S.A., WIN news, Mama Mia, Oprah.com, NineMSN, ABC Radio, 2SM Radio, The Daily Mail, and many others. She is the #1 best-selling author of *From Broke to BMW in 18 months: Your Step by Step Guide to Breaking Through Your Barriers to Achieve The Life You Deserve* and *Your Life Your Purpose: Awakening Your Inner Purpose to Ensure You Live a Fulfilled Life.*

Shar is a regular speaker on select P&O Cruise Lines and at many other events globally. She has been awarded the G*old International Stevie Award, Woman of the Decade in Personal Leadership Award*, and the *Queensland Business Excellence Award*. Her previous publication *YMag®️* was also a finalist in the *Australian Small Business Champion Awards.* When she isn't getting prepared to be in the Hollywood Swag Bags at the 2023 Oscars, she is continuing her global mission of guiding women to be seen, heard, and remembered. www.sharmoore.com.au

Be all of you!

11

THE WEALTH OF PERSONAL FULFILLMENT

BY TARRYN REEVES

*"All the money in the world doesn't mean a thing
if you don't have the time to enjoy it."*

- OPRAH

I don't really view myself as the traditional wealth-driven person, because what is wealth anyway? What does it look like? I personally value meaning and fulfillment most.

As humans, we are consuming machines. We're always trying to upgrade our homes, phones, and faces - it's madness. Do you ever stop to think about why you may be acquiring so much? Are you upgrading all these things because they enrich you or because you want to feel better about yourself? There's nothing wrong with buying what you desire, but what I'm trying to ask here is, what else are you doing to find fulfillment?

111

More than Money

Wealth isn't just about money - it's the decisions you make, how you choose to spend your time, and how you nurture your relationships, and yourself. It's the freedom to choose where you exert your freedom of choice.

I'm no better than you. I used to spend so much money on books and courses, and when I'd do so, I knew my indulgent and sometimes addictive behavior was highlighting the neglect in taking care of myself. When I felt the most stressed or anxious, I'd turn to acquiring things, and it was instant dopamine. There was a sigh of relief with each purchase, but the hunger was never sated, nor was it sustainable. This was one of those moments in life where I looked at myself and asked what else can I do? What else can people contribute to extend and balance those feel-good hormones?

Selfless Steps

The way that I see it, wealth is an infinity symbol cycle, and paying it forward, in my opinion, is our responsibility. I realized the quick fixes of endorphin releases were able to be prolonged in a healthy manner when I took more selfless steps. The selflessness turned into my own form of activism, which I share in my message and in what I do, in order to encourage others to do their part as beings of this Earth.

My most recent brand addition to my company umbrella is *Four Eagles Publishing*. The platform is for high-level entrepreneurs to find their voice through storytelling and create ripple effects of impact across the globe. Then there is *Zimpasha*, my creative marketing, virtual assistance, and web development agency designed to support others to create businesses that fulfill them and contribute to the world around them.

Fully You

My third business is my personal brand, Tarryn Reeves. I do intuitive business coaching, agency work, and publishing - but where I truly shine, is through my out-of-the-box and unconventional energy. I like to bring quirkiness, fun, and uniqueness to the table in my business. I'll sometimes even show up in my pajamas to meetings. I'm expressive and authentic, and I pride myself on telling it like it is.

> *"Don't settle for anything less than 'F#$k Yes' across the board."*
>
> **- KATRINA RUTH**

Startup for Women

Part of my brand is connected to my passion for women starting businesses that make an impact. When women make good money, they don't typically run to buy the latest Mustang, yachts, or holiday homes. Women are more conscious forces and invest it back into the community. Women make more ethical choices – whether that is purchasing organically sourced foods or ethically made clothing. We start charities and uplift other women.

I like to see women finding their voices because women tend to tone their voices down to be more palatable. I like to heal that by offering women the outlet to share their stories, write books, or storytelling through their businesses and marketing strategies. Women still need to be wives, mothers, friends, sisters, and themselves at the end of each day, and I want that to be of more discussion. My passion for celebrating women is the tie-in with all three of my businesses. The Tarryn Reeves brand represents all that I stand for - it's all of me.

The Cost of 6 Figures

Before I became a multi-business owner, a wife, and a mother, I was climbing the corporate ladder at 23, making six figures, and thinking I had it made. Society tells you that's what success looks like, but they fail to mention the other side. The other side is where I was exhibiting massive burnout, struggling with anxiety, and dealing with past traumas, all while keeping it together for a job. My self-worth was reflected by what I could achieve, and if I wasn't achieving something then I wasn't good enough. It was as if I couldn't just be. I continue doing the work today of unlearning and reminding myself that it is okay to just be.

Being a Solopreneur

When I first started out as an entrepreneur, I was in a one-person band, which had me booking myself up and burning out quickly. I couldn't simply focus on being the visionary of my business. Today, I find more relief around that conditioning, because I hired the right people to come into my team, for me to continue being that visionary; the power of a team shouldn't be overlooked.

Everything is a choice, and it comes at a cost, whether that is your time, energy, money, or relationships. It's important to identify your boundaries and where you thrive best in your work.

Victory through Vulnerability

I thrive most at my job when I am practicing authenticity. I find that people are always looking for permission to be themselves, and when people see others modeling themselves unapologetically, they feel much safer doing so. Though we like to think that humanity has evolved, to follow is a biologically imprinted behavior. When society tells us that it's okay to be a certain way and not another way, our minds subconsciously tell us that we must not risk getting kicked out of the tribe. It's a survival mechanism and humans are hard-wired to conform.

The world needs more people to realize that they are capable. I used to ride horses and my dad would always say, "If the horse throws you off, and you don't get back on that horse, it learns that it can keep throwing you off." There comes a time when we realize that we cannot lounge in the victim pool forever. You make your way out, and that's a choice. It's about taking the necessary time in doing the necessary work.

Self-Therapy and Storytelling

When my clients come into a writing program with me, it's a transformational writing experience. The stories I teach people to tell are vulnerable and real; ones that they've probably never told anybody before. When I nurture and give them the platform to tell their stories, they see themselves in a different light. I know this because my clients tell me, but I've also personally undergone the powerful journey of telling my own story in *Wild Women Rising, Corporate Dropouts, and Younger Self Letters.*

I wrote about my anxiety in the latter book, and how I used to think that my anxiety made me weak or broken. I went back on my anti-anxiety medication because I wouldn't be able to continue the work in the capacity that I do today. I made the choice to choose more for myself.

I Didn't Die

There's so much fear in whatever you're speaking about, but when you do it, you discover that you didn't die, nor did your business cave, nor does your family hate you. The healing is in meeting that fear face-on, that is when it actually loses its power. Once you communicate your truth and put it out into the world, it's not just your truth, it becomes shared wisdom.

Wealth looks like all these things. It's not strictly one thing – it's your message and how you want to tell it and what you'd like for it to expand. It's the give-back.

I donate 1 percent of my turnover every year to environmental and social causes, which are marketed on my website, because otherwise, what's the point? I'm not a millionaire by any stretch of the imagination and I don't pay myself nearly enough for what I do, but I donate that 1 percent of what I make, because I believe that if I'm not giving back to the planet that I'm living on and the community that I'm living in, it will cease to exist.

I'm not interested in being a preacher, I'm interested in being a teacher. I teach by being the example.

Pregnancy Activation

As a parent, I see how my actions, my words, and my ideologies teach my daughter daily. Being a mother is the hardest, but most rewarding thing I've ever experienced. Pregnancy was my activation: lioness energy came over me and it expelled me from my own victim pool. As parents, we're modeling our behavior unto our children. Kids learn from the people they are surrounded by, and 90% of the time, it's what they see their parents doing every day.

> *"To be poor and be without trees, is to be the most starved human being in the world. To be poor and have trees, is to be completely rich in ways that money can't buy."*

> - CLARISSA PINKOLA ESTES

My Daughter Knows Naughty

When my daughter sees trash on the side of the street she'll say, "Mom these naughty people are killing the Earth, that's not okay!", because she's heard me talk about it and we have these conversations. It's all interwoven with who we are and who we are becoming, whether that is in our business or everyday life. Our choices and what we stand for are being passed on to the next generation. What we teach is what's going to evolve into the next iteration of humanity.

My motto is "Inspire. Impact. Ignite." What we teach is what can be created. The truth is I feel the greatest wealth when I make a list of all the things I have that money can't buy. My experiences and memories are priceless. To be able to choose and prioritize more of these moments is to have wealth beyond measure. This is my truth.

My words are my legacy and it's through my stories, my published works, and the pay it forward policy I live by that generates the greatest abundance for future generations including my daughter. I often think of my life as a living record of something she can live by and be enriched by so that she may have her own wealth in her own way.

I want this for all women not just my daughter but it's through her that I find some of my greatest inspiration. I challenge you to find your inspiration, where you will make your impact, and the people you can ignite in these new ways of wealth.

-Tarryn Reeves

Tarryn Reeves is "The Book Queen" and CEO of *Four Eagles Publishing*, the publishing house of choice for conscious disruptors, visionaries, and leaders. She is a *USA Today* best-selling author, book coach, publisher, and marketer whose work has been featured in the *Los Angeles Times, World News Network, Thrive Global*, and more. Together with her team, she works with high-level entrepreneurs to create best-selling books that act as marketing tools and authority builders that grow their businesses and create ripple effects of impact with their message across the globe.

Hi Melisa,
You are
Resilient!
♡ Blair

12

SHARING TO EMPOWER

BY BLAIR KAPLAN VENABLES

"I learned that real happiness doesn't come from getting but from giving."

- GABRIELLE BERNSTEIN

I thought I'd be a wine-drinking soccer mom of two by now, but at 36, I'm sober, I have no kids, and I love bird-watching – I can thank the global pandemic for that last one. I'm serious. I just started identifying birds one day, with binoculars, hikes, and all. I've come to accept that this isn't the life that I imagined living, but here I am living it because it's the only one I have.

Let's whip through some background information. I was going to be a psychologist, but then I thought, "Holy shit, I have too many problems," which then led me to go into public relations. It was a jump, but it was within a deep philosophical moment that I realized that I'd rather throw parties than help fix people, in the traditional way a psychologist would. With my background in PR came the knowledge of how to hold space for people. I have an empathetic capacity to allow people to feel heard - maybe because growing up, I wasn't very heard. I was a child of divorce. Nobody told me my dad was living with addiction, so I just assumed my dad didn't love me anymore. Imagine being a daddy's girl and your dad stops coming around. If someone would have told me, "Hey, he's sick, but he loves you anyway, he just can't show up because he's not well," perhaps that would have been a different narrative in my head.

My last drink was on December 31, 2018. I began my life of sobriety the next day, January 1, 2019. That day, I awoke to a letter from my dad, apologizing for what had happened during my formative years and explaining his addiction to me.

My Father's Regrets

I'm open and honest about my life. I think people should normalize being more open – which is essentially why I'm here. If I can help people open those floodgates and move them through their challenges, then I feel that I'm doing my life's work. Eventually, my dad and I began to build a new relationship and he even walked me down the aisle. At the end of 2018, we learned that my dad was terminally ill. I felt we were losing our time together, which led my father and me to share our story about forgiveness, addiction, resilience, and essentially our father-daughter story.

The feedback we got was positive; we were really helping people and inspiring them to want to heal, seek therapy or fix relationships in their lives. My dad and I were truly inspired and started building on what we called The Global Resilience Project; a community where people share their stories of resilience. We quickly integrated this idea into a book, featuring many other people's stories about forgiveness, addiction, and strength. I went beyond and have also started the Radical Resilience podcast to give people an additional space to share their stories. My dad and I want this book and our online movement to be a legacy piece.

There are a lot of extremes to my story. The past couple of years has been some of the most turbulent times. In 2019, my grandfather passed away, I was in a car accident where I suffered from a concussion, and my husband had a heart attack and had to undergo quadruple bypass surgery. After suffering from infertility for some time, I became pregnant, but that joy was short-lived when I had a miscarriage in November 2020. About three weeks after, my father-in-law passed away. And by February of 2021, my mother had passed away.

Grief Meets Resilience

My life was changing rapidly. I was in a constant state of grieving. While I was learning about people's stories of resilience through The Global Resilience Project, I was enduring some of the hardest challenges, losses, and traumatic events.

I had started the project because my dad was terminally ill and I wanted to produce something with him in our lifetime together, but while doing so, I lost the most important members of my family. Within 360 days after my mother's death, my dad succumbed to his illness and passed away. I never thought that by the time I'd be wrapping up the first book for The Global Resilience Project, I'd also be grieving my mother, father, and the drastic changes in my life. The Global Resilience Project has become a way for me to turn my pain into purpose. It's a way for us all to practice mental wealth, love, and empowering each other to continue onward.

Bounce Forward

Over the years, I've learned there are certain things to do to strengthen your resilience muscles so when you need them, you can move forward. I used to define resilience as the ability to bounce back, but it is quite the opposite - it's the ability to bounce forward. If you think about it, what are you really bouncing back to? With every challenge or experience, we learn something, and we don't go back to where we were, because we're constantly moving forward to where we are going.

I practice gratitude every day. I've created it into a daily ritual where I list three things I'm grateful for, at the same time, every day. Doing this for 21 days changes the neural pathways in the brain to see the world more positively. I started doing this over six years ago, where I set my phone alarm at 9 p.m., and every day I, alongside my husband or whomever I'm around, list our three things from that day. I call it the Gratitude Alarm and it's a ritual that has helped me through my worst times, because at the end of each day, I'm forced, in a sense, to think about the three things that are great.

I believe that to be brave is to be vulnerable and to be vulnerable is to be brave. I like to show up authentically with an air of "what you see is what you get." If you follow me on social media, that air is very apparent, because I don't hide. I showcase what is happening behind the scenes of my life. I share the challenges, so when people want to work with me, they can truly see what I'm capable of overcoming. I'm not your traditional social media expert, and that's what I've been told people like about me.

Mindset Pioneer

I'm a social media marketing mentor meaning when I work with clients, I work with their mindsets.

I started working in social media marketing before social media marketing was a profession. I've been called a pioneer or an avant-garde maven, but quite simply, I'm a storyteller and I use social media to get the stories of my clients out there. There is a certain way to go into sharing your story, and I've got it down to a science. It's a model that I've been modifying for 15 years now but started promoting only a year ago. It's helped me in the way that I present, market, and share my world. It's called the Social Media Empowerment Pillar, aka EMPOWER.

EMPOWER

1. **Edutain**: Building content that is both educating and entertaining.

2. **Money**: What is your advertising budget? How much do you want to make? Get specific with your money goals.

3. **Personas**: Make content to attract your ideal customer. Who do you wish there was more of? Create a persona for those people.

4. **Other Players**: I believe in collaboration over competition. Who are your potential partners? Where are they getting PR? Maybe there's an opportunity for you to be somewhere they're not.

5. **Wins**: People don't show their wins enough. If you don't share what you're capable of, how will others know what you're capable of? How will your community support you if they can't brag about you? I call it "peacocking" and bragging to the public. Here is where you can build your publicity strategy and get media coverage by pitching your wins to journalists and beyond. Have your expertise featured in publications, so when people find you, they know that you are credible.

6. **Engagement**: Show people you're a real person behind your social media. You can't just post and ghost. Keep commenting, following, and liking. It's important to interact with your crowd.

7. **Realistic Goals**: I'm all about setting goals; personal, professional, and health. If you don't know where you're going, how are you going to get there? How much money do you want to make? How much content do you want to put out? What type of content are you going to put out? How much money do you want to invest in putting out that content? Where do you want to go next?

These seven pillars are the essence of cultivating clout and becoming a thought leader. I think the most important thing to remember during building your social media presence, is to show up authentically with your story. Don't worry about posting a certain number of times a day. In fact, I say, "Eff the Algo!" (I created a workshop with the same name). Show up as you are. It's not always about getting 5,000 likes. Surely, you can Google how to make a post, but do you know how to tell your story and empower others? Ask yourself, "Do I know what my story is?"

As mentioned, I'm not one for the traditional. I have been compared to Gabby Bernstein, Brené Brown, and Tony Robbins and have been told that I have a comedic personality compared to Amy Schumer. I have spoken at events with renowned individuals like Bob Proctor, Les Brown, Brian Tracy, and Denis Waitley while being called an "up and coming thought leader."

Millions Empowered

My goal remains to be a strong and encouraging force. I want to always be empowering millions of people on a consistent basis. Funny enough, I told myself on my 36th birthday, back in August, that by the time I'm 40, I want to empower eight million people. I was then booked on a TV show where viewership was 15 million. I then thought, "Well, I guess I gotta set a higher goal!" So, I've humbly bumped that goal up to 88 million people.

I'm only just a vintage millennial...And i'm just at the beginning of my journey.

-Blair Kaplan Venables

Blair Kaplan Venables is an expert in social media marketing and the president of Blair Kaplan Communications, a British Columbia-based PR agency. She brings fifteen years of experience to her clients which include global wellness, entertainment, and lifestyle brands. She is the creator of the Social Media Empowerment Pillars, has helped her customers grow their followers into the tens of thousands in just one month, win integrative marketing awards, and more. Blair is listed in *USA Today* as one of the Top 10 Conscious Female Leaders to Watch in 2022, and Yahoo! listed Blair as a Top Ten Social Media Expert to Watch in 2021. She has spoken on national stages and her expertise has been featured in media outlets including *Forbes, CBC Radio, Entrepreneur and Thrive Global*. Blair is a best-selling author and her forthcoming book, *The Global Resilience Project* will be published in 2022. She is the co-host of the *Dissecting Success* podcast and in her free time, you can find Blair growing *The Global Resilience Project's* online community where users share their stories of overcoming life's most difficult moments.

13

A BEAUTIFUL LIFE

BY ADRIANA MONIQUE ALVAREZ

*"When you want something, all the Universe
conspires in helping you achieve it."*

- PAULO COELHO

Born and raised in a rural farming community a
long way from nowhere, everyone knew me. I was
Vernon and Dyanna's daughter and if someone didn't
make that connection all I had to do was to mention
my grandparents. At a young age, I understood what
money could provide even if I didn't see it from an adult
perspective.

My grandpa had been a truck driver, miner, and
flailing entrepreneur before he struck gold. He decided
to start a lumber business in the late seventies and that
became the cash cow he had been searching for. Within
ten years my young parents went from bouncing checks
to building a new house. My bedroom had one wall
with the softest pink tulip wallpaper with a bedspread to
match. I had a big closet and en-suite bathroom. I was in

heaven! I had an appreciation for the finer things in life. What I discovered in my childhood was how much money would reveal about people.

It didn't take long for the small town to become a glasshouse. In the 5th grade, my teacher announced we were going to have a Valentine's Day party and card exchange. My mom took me to pick out cards and I carefully wrote one out to every kid in my class. The next day I was dressed up as I proudly walked into class with my box full of love notes. When it was Elaine's turn, she walked around the room and placed a white envelope on each desk. As she approached me, she said loud enough for the entire class to hear, "Your parents can buy you a Valentine, they are rich enough!"

Early Embarrassment

I could feel my face turn red and that was the day I learned not everyone was going to be happy about my good fortune. The older I got the more I wanted to leave my little Mayberry. I began to withdraw in high school and instead of going to parties I was filling notebooks full of all the places I wanted to see. In my senior year, I graduated a semester early and nothing gave me more relief than no longer walking the halls of MCHS.

Everyone expected me to go to college, get a degree and marry the neighbor. I left the most beautiful nest a child could ask for, only a few months after graduating. My heart ached with homesickness, but I knew it was time for me to fly.

I went to central Florida to attend a four-week boot camp that would teach me how to live off the grid, without electricity or plumbing. I was taught a crash course on how to grow a garden, raise animals and butcher them. I learned how to figure it out no matter what circumstances I encountered. I am sure everyone thought this spoiled girl would fall flat on her face, but I absolutely loved it. I went to bed with the sun and fell in love with the goat of which I was in charge. I made bread better than I ever thought I could and one night as we were talking over dinner one lady mentioned the Kosovo Crisis and that the state-run orphanage needed a full-time volunteer. I remember instantly knowing, that I was their person. I asked to be connected and within a few months, I was packing my bags for Tirana, Albania. This is the point where everyone Googles Albania because even though it's right next to Greece and Italy, very few people know anything about this obscure and endearing country.

Dance, Swim

I spent the summer with the kids on the Adriatic Sea. We slept in an abandoned building and ate cucumbers and tomatoes for breakfast. The kids loved to swim all day and dance at night. The water was clear and calm, and I had never experienced this kind of raw beauty. I was in a whole new world, and I was literally living my teenage dream.

At the end of the summer, I returned to Colorado and made the decision to move to Tirana, Albania to live with 120 kids in the orphanage. I raised money and asked for

133

the support of my community. I flew out with eight duffle bags stuffed full of clothes, toiletries, and toys. My mom helped me get settled and when it was time for her to go, I cried for days. It was my turn to give back and to be the rock my parents had always been for me.

Questions, Despair

I remember my head hurting from hearing the Albanian language all day long. No one is a better teacher than a child and within three months I was able to communicate with them. By the time winter had arrived I found myself sobbing every minute there was not a child around me. I had got to know them, and my heart was broken. Most of the kids didn't have either parent or some had been separated from their siblings. One night I buried my head in my pillow and I said, "What am I doing here? I have no formal training to help these kids with the pain they have been through. I cannot save them. I cannot go back and change their past. I cannot lift the sadness of this country for all it has been through. What can I actually do for them?"

That is when I heard the still small voice that would become my Guide for life. It said, "No, you cannot save them or fix the bigger issues this country or these children are facing. What you can do is create small moments of joy with them. What you can do is love them. What you must do is look for the beauty in each moment." That became my only focus, my full-time job. One day I found a little old man selling popcorn in the city center. I walked the kids down and we had a great time playing and eating popcorn. For Christmas, I threw them a party and we danced all night.

When they got hurt, I hugged them. And when they laughed, I laughed with them.

Defining My Life

After three years I went on to do the same at an HIV baby orphanage in Nairobi, Kenya. What no one could have known was how these experiences perfectly prepared me for the life I have now. A year later when I met my husband Derek on a blind date and we quickly became engaged to be married I asked him for one thing, that we create a beautiful life. I told him I didn't want him to have a good job or make lots of money if it meant leaving our home for eight, ten, or even twelve hours a day. I told him I'd rather live in our car than become the kind of people who didn't share meals around the table.

I never dreamt of owning a business, but I always dreamt of having a beautiful life. This became the litmus test for every decision we made. We didn't look at a project or client and ask if it would provide an income, we asked ourselves if the way we were approaching our life and business would create a good life. Over and over, we made decisions that probably didn't make any sense to those on the outside, but we simply weren't interested in trade-offs that would lead to us forgetting what matters most.

When we added babies to the mix and our family grew, this became even more important. Nothing asks me to get my priorities straight like the loving faces of two boys. I could feel them watching our every move and more importantly I could feel the influence we had in their lives. If these boys became us, would that be a good or bad thing? Derek and I took them to see the world right after they were born. We worked a few days and filled most of our days with adventures most only dream of. They have played in Frida Kahlo's courtyard. Cheered at the Day of the Dead parade in Mexico City. Chased the waves in Costa Rica. Stuffed themselves with Greek yogurt and honey. Celebrated Easter at the Vatican. Spent the summer at Lake Como. Felt like kings in Dubrovnik. Ran around the monasteries of Montenegro. And spent countless summer days in the gentle waters of the Adriatic Sea. When the world changed, I spent three months grieving and soul searching. I knew the only thing that mattered was to return to my little Mayberry and give them the childhood I had.

Ripening

We drove four days out of the Yucatan to Colorado and when we pulled into my grandparent's driveway, I knew without a shadow of a doubt we were home. The piano my Papa C.R. gave me was in the living room. Derek's art was on the walls. The same fridge I used to get snacks from was still in the kitchen. We now work a few days and spend the rest renovating the house and property. Check on the plums and peaches to see if they are ripe yet. Plant hundreds of tulips and daffodils for Spring. Fill the pantry with healthy food. Add to the orchard and plan the greenhouse. Put ladybugs in the herbs garden.

When the world doesn't make sense and my heart feels heavy, I remember what I heard in that cold, concrete room in the orphanage. While I can't fix the bigger issues of our world and I can't save us from what is unfolding, I can create moments of joy. I can make chocolate soufflé for breakfast. I can color with the boys and pray for them at bedtime. I can let Derek hold me on the couch. And I can invite my parents over for dinner.

A Rich, Beautiful Life

A beautiful life has always been synonymous with a rich life for me. Society would love to sell us all on something that looks like going into debt for higher education, climbing corporate ladders while selling our souls, and filling our homes with stuff that we don't have time to enjoy. It is our job to ask, is this what I always dreamt of? Is this what lasts? And what will matter when I'm eighty-eight years old looking back over my life?

What about you? What is the dream that you have held in your heart? It doesn't have to make sense to anyone except you. There were many times my path didn't make any sense, but it was perfect, nevertheless. I am sure that once you commit to it and love it, many amazing people will find a way to be part of it. If you haven't expressed what is in your heart, I encourage you to use your voice to share it with someone. I have found that sharing it with a stranger is sometimes easier than with those who love us most since they will naturally try to protect us. I know firsthand the fear of sharing a dream. While there is a chance some people won't agree, there will be many who do and feel encouraged by hearing your vision.

If you're not ready to say it out loud, it's quite alright to start with writing it down and filling journals with your dreams.

No Validation

What if the whole world no longer needed the validation of letters behind their name, the applause of another, or a certain number in the bank account to make them worthy? We just might have a world that values health, relationships, and watching the sunset with a grateful heart. This is true wealth in my book.

-Adriana Monique Alvarez

Adriana Monique Alvarez is the CEO and Founder of AMA Publishing. She teaches women how to start highly profitable publishing companies and has written, *How to Start a Six Figure Publishing Company* that is available on Amazon. She's a *USA Today* bestselling author and her most recent book, *The Younger Self Letters* debuted #1 on bestseller lists internationally. She has been seen in *Forbes, Huffington Post, International Living, America Daily Post, Daily Grind, Addicted2Success, Elephant Journal, London Daily Post, Entrepreneur*, FOX, ABC, and NBC. She is currently living in the middle of nowhere Colorado where she is renovating her grandparents´ home and learning how to homestead with her husband Derek, and two sons, Sam and Grant.

14

NURTURING SUCCESS

BY EBONY SWANK

"Define success in your own terms, achieve it by your own rules, and build a life you're proud to live."

- ANNE SWEENEY

A simple truth I try to instill in my daughters, and by extension my company, is for women to be unapologetically themselves, to embrace who they are. Life's too short to be ashamed of the choices we make and the circumstances that led to them. I don't take losses lying down. Every setback and every failure are an opportunity for me to strategically plan my next move. My failures are what nurtured my success. And I want *Swank A Posh* to embody that. For me, wealth is more than financial. It's the quality of our character, and the passion we pour into our work. Wealth provides a measure of freedom.

What we do with that freedom, who we really are, who we want to be, has a way of revealing itself.

Being a Black woman in America, and all the culture, history, and pain that comes with it – I knew I had a high mountain to climb. It was important for me to give these voiceless, often ignored women a platform to showcase their beauty. Especially when we are so often mocked and ridiculed for just being who we are – authentic. That's what it means to be unapologetic: to stand secure in your own identity in a room full of people looking at you like you're the problem.

In the realm of fast fashion, trends are inspired by what's happening on the runway. You have a brief period of time before a trend fades and is replaced by a new one. I didn't want *Swank* to be labeled as something so superficial. I wanted my creative mind and business to thrive. Our pieces are inspired by designers and artists all over the fashion world. I'm happy to design products with vendors and portions of *Swank's* catalog. Everything I sell is everything I've touched.

Trends, Versatility

Versatility is what I strive for when creating pieces. It's not uncommon for women to wear shorts or tank tops in colder weather. This is why I'll create a piece that can be worn year-round. I don't shy away from trends, though. In fact, they're helpful. On Instagram, waist wraps were growing in popularity, and I saw a market for them and launched my own wraps. I put my personal touch on them, so it's not only unique to *Swank* but specific to my audience. For any entrepreneur, you must know where a particular market or demographic is leaning, especially in fashion. Knowing what trends are becoming everyday staples can give you the leverage to maximize profit and satisfy customers.

Therefore learning from failures is so important.

During the tail-end of 2009's recession, I came up with the idea for *Swank* and opened my first store of that year. At the time, I didn't think it would turn into a full-time career. I was trying to make ends meet for my daughter and me. In those early years, I learned quickly that life doesn't stop for anyone. The clothes I was selling weren't turning a profit. The money I made was paying the rent, not running a business. Around this time, I found out I was pregnant with my second daughter. Eventually, I couldn't afford to keep my store open. I closed *Swank's* doors, and shortly after, my mother had a heart attack.

Resilient Mothers

To be a black mother is to be resilient. The sacrifices we make for our children are great. We sweat, bleed, and give up so much of ourselves so they can have the comfort we didn't. We cultivate their future and happiness and pray our efforts are enough to compensate for our mistakes. My mother was no different. Her love and unconditional support were a constant I relied upon. She helped me raise my daughters.

When my mom had her heart attack, I didn't think she would make it. The doctors explained the blood flow was obstructed, and she would need triple bypass surgery if she had any hope to recover. The realization my mom was dying wasn't anything I could prepare for. I felt robbed, she was being snatched from me, and I didn't have the time I needed with her. During the hardest fights in my life, she was my rock. Here I was, going through something so painful, and my security was disrupted.

When faced with death, you realize so many things in life don't matter. Chasing luxury and having a "grind" mindset for the sake of it is misplaced vanity if it's not rooted in something bigger than yourself. There are only a few good things in life that are important. I credit these good things to God. He's maneuvered situations for me, and I've felt his hand in my life more times than I can count. All I wanted was my mother, and I would exchange anything for her. I asked God to sacrifice my unborn child just so I could have more time with her.

No Rest

Ultimately, my mom's bypass surgery was successful. A few months later, I gave birth to my daughter. I was allowed to keep both. I flew my mom from Missouri to live with me full time. After my daughter was born, I would be back in the hospital a week later. My daughter had Intestinal Malrotation, a condition that causes the intestines to twist during the early stages of pregnancy. She would need surgery. I needed rest, but my daughter was my priority. I wouldn't let her go through this alone.

My business was on my mind, too. Twelve-thousand dollars in savings, and I was paying my mom's bills with two young kids. I knew the money would run out quickly if I didn't plan my next move carefully. I wanted my daughter home. The sleepless nights, the back and forth with doctors, and the uncertainty of everything made my blood boil. I was frustrated, but I needed to know what I would do with this business.

Renewed, Reopened

When the doctors gave me the clear, I took my baby home and began scouting locations to reopen *Swank*. With my mom's support, I went to work.

I had some leftover inventory from before, but I needed fresh material to work with. I boarded a plane to Los Angeles with my oldest daughter and sought out vendors. With hopes and prayers, I exceeded my own expectations. I had a profitable business that saw no end to its growth. My family was taken care of, too. In 2018, my mom died. I was willing to sacrifice so much for her. What God gave me, and what I needed, was time. Time with my mother. Time for my daughters to get to know and love their grandmother. Time for me to build a secure life for my children. My mom played a vital role in my initial success. Without her help, I wouldn't be here.

Today, *Swank* has two storefronts in Metro Detroit. I took twelve-thousand dollars and turned it into a forty-million-dollar company. *Swank's* first store, located in a mall next to a Nordstrom, taught me what I needed to be successful. The biggest takeaway is that learning never stops. Still, that first store makes me sick, but I'm not mad about it. I don't know how something so integral to my company remains such a stench I can't shake whenever I visit that mall, even after all this time.

Yet it was key to many of my blessings.

Being featured in *Forbes* magazine put my company full center of the public eye. Success is surrounding yourself with great people. My husband, Tony, and daughters, Alaya and Bailei, give me their unconditional love and support. Mike, my broker, runs my warehouse in Los Angeles and negotiates deals with vendors. No one knows who I am there. Neither do they know I run a multi-million-dollar company. When making large orders, I'm sometimes rejected by store owners. In these times, it's Mike who ensures the vendors are as productive as possible when some don't take me, a black woman, seriously. I value having members like Mike on my team. These people are dedicated and will always stand by me, regardless of my success.

Everyday Women

I take pride in having *Swanks* models resemble everyday women. I am an observer. I know the media pushes for one kind of woman, leaving millions of beautiful women underrepresented. For the aspiring entrepreneur, the best advice I can give is to make sure your product stands out. I made sure I was different, from the flyers to the branding. If you're learning from your product and what you're putting out in the world, you'll find success. If the effort is there, the results will be, too. For me, that was going on Facebook and friending people in my area. I knew they would follow back or, at the very least, see my page if I tagged them. I posted women trying on jeans on Instagram. Which, in a way, became my own form of clickbait. That encouraged more sales from these visual try-ons.

As a businesswoman, it's important to pay attention to what's going on in the realm of the customer. And sometimes that's rejecting offers. I was approached by investors who offered me a million-dollar deal for fifty percent of my company back in 2019. I had sacrificed so much of my heart and energy into Swank, I refused to toss half of it away to out-of-touch investors who didn't know how to navigate my consumer, my community.

Looking back, I can say I never let pain paralyze me. I can't. 50-Cent summed it up best, "Every negative is a positive. The bad things happen to me, I somehow make them good. That means you can't do anything to hurt me." I live by that. Failure will always be temporary if that's at the forefront of everything I do. My work, my ambition, will be what stands. At the end of it all, I guess that's enough.

-Ebony Swank

For over a decade, Ebony Swank has been the Founder and CEO of *Swank A Posh*, a women's clothing boutique that has grown into an 8 figure establishment. She has been featured in *Forbes, Business Deccan, Rolling Out, Black Enterprise*, and countless other publications. A Detroit Native, she single-handedly aids women to be confident in their own skin.

Ebony has done everything from taking the big leap and investing her last $12,000 to start her business, to employing young black women and mentoring them to become executives at *Swank A Posh* or to be owners of their own businesses, or both.

15

FROM TRAGEDY TO TRIUMPH THROUGH SERVICE AND GRATITUDE

BY BARBIE LAYTON

"Want to be wealthy?" Happy? Peaceful?" Say, thank you. It's that simple."

- KEN HONDA

This may come as a shock, but it is okay to have nice things! It is okay to indulge! For example, I have chocolate in my freezer from all over the world, and I realize that I don't crave chocolate because I understand that I can have it whenever I want. When we want what we think we cannot have, it creates a dent in our abundant mindsets. Indulging in that thing you want is completely valid because doing so on occasion isn't going to be bad for you. It's healthier for our current and future selves to allow and accept the opportunities to feel good.

When we allow those moments, our flow understands that we have great worth; this is amplified by what makes us feel good and we will naturally be engaged to bring more great things into our lives.

I consciously decided to use fashion as a form of therapy when I was diagnosed with a chronic illness back in 2016. This fashion coping strategy saved me. Before that diagnosis, I had already survived three near-death experiences and yet continued to be active. Travel was my passion, and I loved to experience new cultures. I had enjoyed two international trips a year, lived on three continents, had visited over 35 countries, plus most of the United States, and the Hawaiian Islands.

At the time of the diagnosis, I was single, working every day, and after work, homebound, on the couch with an ice pack due to excruciating pain. Sometimes my pain would be so intense that I made my fashion therapy a mathematical formula. I thoroughly enjoy giving myself the time to do my makeup and put on an outfit that makes me feel good. There were days when my pain/energy would make me feel like a volume 2 and I intentionally chose fashion that could be at volume 10, and they would make me feel like I was at volume 6, and I would find myself feeling better.

Exterior Shell

I started experimenting with different styles, hair, makeup, and designer brands. I was pulled toward amplifying my exterior shell because I realized that when you're faced with your own mortality and the belief that you might die soon, you see that you've kept all the good stuff locked away. I compare it to when you visit your grandmother's house and she'd place plastic sheets over her nice furniture to keep them in pristine condition, but never genuinely enjoying the luxury of her space. What's the point of having a couch if you don't allow yourself to sit on the comfortable cushion? I took this instance and ran in the opposite direction.

I figured then, that if I was going to die, I might as well enjoy my wealth while I was alive. It was like supreme fashion saved my life. Since I dressed intentionally, I would be fully decked out on a Tuesday, and when I went to Costco, I would find I would suddenly have a personal shopper, or get an extra VIP experience or bonuses when I showed up like that. It was such an uncanny thing, that people were serving me in such a beautiful way, and I was so grateful as it was a different way to be received.

VIP Mindset

I landed upon an empowering perspective: you are the VIP of your own life. You are the person that should be pulling out the best perfume and the best China set, and not saving it for show. I imagine money as an energy and it's something you can play with. When you continue to think in lack, you will only go in that direction. However, this is an unlimited universe with a plethora of abundance, and many people in their scarcity mindset have not been able to step into that. I'm very big on shifting your mindset, and when we have an abundance mindset, we inspire the wealth that comes our way. It's like flying at the airport.

When you gain access to VIP lounges in airports, they have amenities and smoked glass and no signs, unless you're in the know. It's like magical doors opening for you that you never knew existed!

Gamification

Then in 2017, I remember seeing a host on MTV: Total Request Live, wearing a Louis Vuitton x Supreme jacket, and I adored it. Somebody told me it costs $6,000, which was absurd to me, but then through further educating myself, I understood that streetwear became a subculture and had people waiting in lines to get a taste. It was literally like its own language. I was so intrigued, which got me to start doing something I call *gamification*; I essentially made finding and buying certain designer gems into my own little game.

There was a time I was able to get my hands on the holy grail red and white Supreme hoodie that costs $25,000, and they only make a few per country. They build scarcity into their model to drive up demand. The upside was that I bought it 90% off since I was buying secondhand. The downside was that I had to learn the hard way by purchasing it in five different ways until I bought the real deal (four of them ended up being fake versions).

I'm not chasing that anymore; as a middle-aged Hypebeast, streetwear is not really within my generation sphere, but I've come to appreciate it. I capitalized on the scarcity of the market because it became a treasure hunt, and you must decode the details and see if they fit the original, unique piece. It's like an education to test your limits and I do it out of the pure joy of allowing myself to have nice things.

Although I love to look my best, my messages are never about perfection. It's about when everybody rises together in an unlimited universe, which is when we all can have as much of the pie as we want. I always tell people, "You are your own reality show" - it's about showing up for yourself. These ideas certainly contributed to saving my life, because from this perspective I felt like I had everything I needed, and I was able to manifest the rest.

Frugal, Grateful

I learned an abundant mindset early on, growing up "wealth adjacent" in Malibu, California. I can see the impact of my ancestors' lives on perspectives of wealth. The maternal side of my family originally came from wealth traced back to the 1300s that was taken during World War II, and they escaped with what they could carry. My grandmother spoke nine languages, and they were immigrants to two new countries. They saw all work as an opportunity and my grandfather even worked into his 70s.

On the other side of my family, my grandparents were originally from the Midwest and my grandma was an Oklahoma beauty queen who met my grandfather during World War II at a bomb munitions plant.

They had survived the Great Depression, so they were always very frugal, except when it came to the quality of food for holidays. My parents met on the beach in Malibu, as my father was an O.G. Surfer in the '60s, and my mother was a cute blond from Germany.

My mom was a genius at stretching a dollar! We used to go to garage sales in the wealthy neighborhoods and get all kinds of things like art or tens of thousands of dollars' worth of designer shoes in a bag for $20.00! Consignment stores are still one of my favorite places! I had everything I wanted materially, even if it was last year's model. The phrase rings true: one woman's trash is another woman's treasure.

All things that you consider your abundance, come from your perspective. Our family always had the nicest things but at very discounted prices. I was told that although we lived in a beautiful home, we were the poorest kids on the block. So, we shared chores and did all our gardening ourselves, and didn't have a maid like most of my friends. I did most of the cooking, laundry, and shopping. I could also make a budget and it all taught me responsibility. I was truly grateful for this perspective I was given.

Super-Connector

What I learned growing up gave me a strong foundation of hard work and gratitude. As a kid, I was service-oriented and as a teen, I volunteered at Los Ninos children's charity in Tijuana, Mexico. I put my heart into other community service projects, and this continued into adulthood. I volunteered at the animal shelter and spent five years at my university reading grad papers to help support myself. Working hard, doing what I had to do, and looking for ways to help along the way. I always wanted to add value to my communities and enrich others, and it seems that being a super-connector is in my blood.

Now, I host the program *You Are Amazing* on the Best You TV, which has brought forth 20 countries in participating with my *Kindness Revolution*. The *Kindness Revolution's* mission is to dispel stereotypes and honor each person's journey. It's about finding common ground without media-influenced narratives to bring forth stories and discussions that are authentic, empowering, and ultimately relatable. I believe in the power of unity through kindness, especially amongst women. When women band together, without competing but by lifting each other up from the heart space, it can be so powerful. It's in the collaboration and co-creation where we can positively change and truly come through for one another.

Needs, Wants

In Maslow's *Hierarchy of Needs*, he explains what we have in common: needing to be seen, heard, loved, and accepted. With clients, I keep that at the forefront, because everybody wants and needs the same things. As an intuitive consultant, mentor, and speaker, I help people fall in love with themselves by reflecting themselves to them. I show them how to tap into their flow of abundant energy, their worth, abilities, and all of the love within their grasp.

I think of myself as a heart-centered person and talk to everyone as if they are my equal. Although I may dress up and present as an important person, I thank people who help me and ask people how their day is going, because approaching with kindness is a priceless act. Kindness also gives people the opportunity to reciprocate it back to you.

I want to allow others to uplevel their wealth. My goal around the *Kindness Revolution* was inspired by one of my favorite mantras: the more that I have, the more that I can share. My goal is to continue accessing large spaces and networks to bring my wisdom and compassion to the masses. I value being able to connect with different communities and cultures.

My show was originally born out of honoring my mentors, like Vishen Lakhiani, Naveen Jain, who encouraged me to be bold, Ken Honda, the Zen Millionaire, who talks about happy money and clearing money wounds and thanking the money that you give and get. Today, when I pay my bills or when I have money come in, I say, "Thank you!". He calls it the "Arigato in and Arigato out" and it's all about thanking everything you have and staying in the gratitude frequency.

Go Extreme

During the pandemic, participants of The Best You Expos responded positively to what I call Extreme Gratitude. I had people messaging me that it kept them calm, and preserved their sanity, as it was such an easy reframe. I told people to thank their car, toilet, shower, stove, sink, bed, the roof over their head – you name it. They also thanked the electric company and internet providers who are keeping the lights on and allowing them to work from home. There was a dramatic shift in perspective when people stacked up about twenty things for which to have gratitude! They didn't sit around complaining about what they don't have, because they were able to focus on the multiple people and things that are supporting their livelihood to do what they need to do.

Exalted Wealth

The biggest gift to give the world simply comes down to living and being authentically you, because there is wealth in presenting the truest version of yourself. If you do acquire all kinds of wealth, whether tangible or immaterial, it won't mean a thing if you don't pay it forward. When we believe in the power that is in the reciprocity of giving, and operate from the purity of service, generosity, and giving for giving sake, that is wealth in its most exalted form.

Wealth is something that allows you to have freedom. My philosophy on wealth is about allowing yourself to come into a flow where you feel like you can have whatever you want and for it to be at the same wavelength as you, for you to manifest it into your existence.

Wealth to me means financial freedom plus deep connections that I have made with other heart-centered conscious entrepreneurs.

I hope you find your own definition of wealth and step into your own greatness.

-Barbie Layton

Barbie Layton is best known for helping CEOs and individuals reanimate their dreams and fall in love with themselves. She has been featured in *Big Time Daily, Hollywood Digest, The Entrepreneur Magazine, Forbes*, and other outlets. Barbie hosts the program *You Are Amazing* on the Best You TV.

Barbie is also a leader in Ken Honda's Arigato Community, a member of the *Los Angeles Tribune* VIP Mastermind group, and a recent graduate of Vishen Lakhiani's exclusive MindValley Premium Coaching. She was also nominated for the inaugural Tony Hsieh Award in 2020 and is a member of Keith Ferrazzi's Founder's Group. She has done everything from getting her M.A. in Spiritual Psychology from the University of Santa Monica to participating in the 2007 Cannes film festival's winning documentary about women serving life sentences in Chowchilla, California on *The Prison Project*. When she isn't flexing her 25 years of speaking experience on the main stage, she is recording episodes for her channel on Rhonda Swan's *Get Wild Network*. Barbie is also part of *Can You Really Think and Grow Rich* tour.

16

VISUALIZE SUCCESS

BY APRIL RYAN

"Remember that your real wealth can be measured not by what you have, but by what you are."

- NAPOLEON HILL

I want to start by saying that 80% of my life is my work. From the earliest ages of my life, I've gravitated toward the beauty industry. I've seen my successes come to life, which have all stemmed from my soul's desire for more. More wealth. More security. More opportunities.

I come from a poor upbringing; born in Nadym, Russia, and raised in the small town of Salsk. My mother raised me to always explore my creative side - always being the most encouraging of my artistic ventures. I didn't have a lot of opportunities growing up poor, which helped me get more and more creative with whatever I had access to.

It's wild to think that the once young girl, who was sitting amongst her classmates, creating mini nail designs, grew up to be at the helm of a million-dollar beauty business today. And it's not just any business, it's the very space that I've put my all into. I call it Red Iguana, cheekily named after my favorite pet.

I initially started my journey in the beauty industry as a teenager taking cosmetology classes and learning from professional nail techs. I was artistic growing up, much like my mom pushed me to be, but it wasn't long until I found my passion in business, nor was it long until I became a salon owner myself. I eventually made my way to the U.S. where I was able to really launch my business.

Today, I can confidently say that Red Iguana serves up the best in the beauty market, using only the highest quality ingredients in all our products. It's my first rule because I found not many companies care about the harmful chemicals their customers are putting on their bodies. By considering the best ingredients for my people, Red Iguana has truly been able to penetrate a highly competitive market.

Inventing

My company is also known for an invention that has allowed aspiring nail technicians around the globe to hone their skills. The idea came from personally experiencing the inconveniences of asking to get someone on a consistent basis to be a hand model upon whom to practice, so I figured a practical approach was to invent a tool that nail technician trainees can all use - Red Iguana's very own and first on the market, Silicone

Practice Hands. It's such a fantastic idea that even Chinese vendors produce their dupes of my greatest invention (China seems to always find a way to do that huh?), and that doesn't really bother me. Why? My customers and the audience to which I cater, know that Red Iguana is the most real of real deals, making them the best content daily on social media.

That's another thing that I do as a business owner. While creating and launching high-quality tools and products, I also create my own content and produce engaging visuals and information about new launches to interact with my audience and future customers. Being a prolific content creator has grown Red Iguana's designer brand name and high reputation immensely. I'll say it again - 80% of my life is my work.

Calm Introvert

Let's stray away from all the business talk for a moment. I want to bring forth a little bit about the other 20% of my life. It's a calmer 20%. I'm a huge introvert really. I like to read and gain self-knowledge through YouTube videos like John Kehoe's "Mind Power", *The Secret* by Rhonda Byrne, and *Today's Action, Tomorrow's Wealth* by Sam Rossi - the very book that has educated me to get out of my comfortable introversion and knowing how to talk to millionaires and various important heads in my industry. These smaller habits have allowed me to face some of my hardest days and reap my perpetual successes.

I want to share a small secret about how those hard days are conquered with positivity. Allow me to start by saying that, for the most part, I like to think that much of my success is thanks to a hidden skill that anybody can tap into. It's called visualization. You may have heard of it; it's closely associated with the Law of Attraction and manifesting. I guess I can say that I started visualizing at a young age when I was daydreaming about success and wealth, but the difference between visualizing and daydreaming is the intention aspect.

Visualization Rituals

Today, I intentionally visualize all the things that I want, especially when I'm in a meditative state, which can be anywhere from yoga, working out, or any activity that I feel most focused and raw. In the morning when I do my yoga, I start my visualization ritual by thinking of all the things that I am grateful for. I then mentally picture all the things that I want to bring into my life, whether that be a new car or my dream penthouse in New York City.

I like to incorporate mantras or confidence-boosting affirmations that can also be used if you ever find yourself having a tough time picturing things in your mind. For example, sometimes when I'm in the middle of my workout, I fixate on my own gaze in the mirror, and with each bicep curl, I say to myself, "I am strong. I am unstoppable. I can achieve anything that I want." When we put our body in a state of physical activity, the mind is clearer and able to plant new seeds. It can be as simple or specific as you'd like them to be. I like to repeat those positive self-talks over and over, in order to develop them into positive thoughts, which eventually become a part of my conscious belief system.

Incorporating visualization and manifestation rituals all started from a simple desire of mine. It's kind of funny when I think about it now, and it's something very small that I manifested so seamlessly. It was the simple idea of going to an expensive grocery store one day and never having to worry about the price of my favorite foods. Being that I grew up poor, I wanted to be in a situation where I could spend on anything that I wanted without having to choose between one or the other. Today, I find myself in that very situation; I can purchase all options without having to choose or worry. When we prioritize a positive daily mindset, while also entertaining thoughts about the things we want, the brain creates ways to get it.

Caution: Cutthroats

A lot goes into success-building and one aspect that may sometimes be overlooked or even taken for granted is your support system and really reflecting on who is a genuine supporter and who is worth keeping around when your business takes off. I learned some hard lessons stepping into the beauty industry. I learned of the industry's competitive nature, which is exciting to me and pushes me to go hard, but I've also seen what it can turn its community members into. Due to how cutthroat this industry can be, it's been hard to know who your friends are; who's going to be there to cheer you on through your successes but also be aware of those who will secretly revel in your down moments when you need their advice.

Fortunately, I have found companionship like no other with a fellow beauty entrepreneur, Analuisa Franklin. We're so close, so genuine, and so there for each other.

It's real with her. She adds to my life in both business and personal sectors of my life. A true rockstar. Another and more obvious support system I have is not only my beautiful and encouraging mother but my amazing husband, Artem. He's so extroverted and energetic. Being around his energy inspires me to come out of my comfort zone as well. I realize that business cannot be done by oneself, and Artem is not only my supporter but a big part of the development of Red Iguana. We built it together and he manages so much of the invisible, background work that goes into running a business. Red Iguana wouldn't exist without him, and I'm forever grateful. Maybe you are thinking of those people in your life right now. I realize that we all need good friends and people to help us, champion, and cheer us on. I cherish my support system, as they love me through my toughest moments and celebrate me on my milestone days.

Physical, Internal

Not only have I found success in the physical world, but I also like to reflect on my internal successes as well. I've uncovered some ideologies that I firmly stand by. Here is my parting advice to you:

- When you go into business, you need to be fearless. Try new things, take that risk.

- When you care about people's opinions, you are not putting yourself first. Haters are going to hate. When people are talking, you're probably doing something right.

I find that this advice has always worked for me. By remembering just these two things, I have filtered out the negativity and given my all to my business from my best and most ample self.

I'm continuing to make big moves with Red Iguana along with a few upcoming projects in the works. I'm always working - whether that be externally or internally. The key is to find balance and be grateful for the abundance in both worlds.

-April Ryan

April Ryan was born in Nadym, Russia. She started as a nail technician at the age of 18. Currently 33 years old, she is the CEO of *Red Iguana*. Not only is *Red Iguana* one of the most well-known nail brands but all their products are made with high-quality ingredients. April invented the globally popular silicone practice hands for nail technicians that have been a game-changer in the industry. April also has a heart for helping and participating in charity activities.

17

FROM A VISION TO A CALLING

BY MICHALE GABRIEL

"Wealth is not a matter of intelligence, it's a matter of inspiration."

- JIM ROHN

"Are you that woman who makes grown men cry?"

"Yes," I said into the phone. "That would be me."

"Can you teach us to do what you do?"

"You mean make grown men cry?"

She laughed. "To communicate like you do. From the heart."

I didn't know it when I took that phone call from The Boeing Company, but my vision for my life as a storyteller was about to change.

I never could have imagined what was coming next.

The path that led me to that call began 15 years earlier. I was 36, running backwards up a hill near my home in Kirkland, Washington, trying to create new neurological brain connections, something I had learned in a recent workshop. Next, I went to my backyard to meditate, a practice I was beginning daily. As my breathing slowed, I found myself entering a place of stillness. In my mind's eye, I saw a globe resting on a pair of hands. The words above it were "Peace through Story."

The image took my breath away and resonated in every cell in my body. I had no idea what it meant, but the directive was clear. I was to go out into the world and create peace through storytelling.

Power of Story

I had just finished directing a successful $2.8 million capital campaign for the School of International Studies at the University of Washington. I used the tool of storytelling to engage new donors for the school. As a former director of children's public library services, I understood the power of stories to activate the imagination, to engage and inspire, but this moment was different. This was a directive from my soul.

I knew immediately that in order to fulfill it, I had to quit my job and follow it full-time. Start my own business. Become a professional storyteller. And figure out how to make a living at it. With no real plan or strategy, I did just that.

I was married at the time, and my spouse and I had made decisions based on two incomes. He was not pleased. Every day when I came home, I'd find him standing at the front door, asking me how much money I'd made. He wasn't the only one: even my brother told me to go and get a "real job." The pressure was intense. I knew that most local storytellers in Seattle had other jobs and did storytelling on the side. Most schools were paying for storytelling performances and school residencies by holding PTA bake sales.

I soon realized that being a full-time professional storyteller was not a financially stable situation. Yet somehow, I knew that if I did this part-time, my calling would not be fully realized. I needed to trust that I would find a way.

Growing Past Fear

In the early years, especially after my decision to divorce, I would look at my calendar, add up the revenue from scheduled storytelling bookings, and become overwhelmed with fear that I wouldn't be able to pay my bills. Sometimes I would lie in the fetal position, unable to get out of bed.

Amazingly, it was during those times I was able to experience the grace and trust that comes from following one's true path. I discovered that to get myself into action, I needed a story big enough to push past my fear. I also discovered that any story I told myself about facing my fear, or my financial circumstances, or shaming or blaming, did not cut it. I would remain in bed, too scared to move.

Finally, I landed on a story that worked. "Michale, here's the deal. You're not the only person who has received a directive from the universe to follow their passion and express their gifts. Yet because they weren't supported, or encouraged, or championed - or they just lacked the courage to act - they are doing something less fulfilling, and the world is the worse for it. If you sacrifice your calling and get a 'real job,' you are affecting not only yourself. You are impacting all those others who at this moment are in the very same place. This is not just about you. It's about them, too. For the sake of all of you, get up and move."

Bold Enough

That was the story that was big enough, bold enough, and inclusive enough to get me to slide to the edge of my bed, place my feet on the floor, stand up, and take action, make calls, send emails, schedule meetings, and write proposals. I knew I was doing this not just for myself, but for others, too. And this story worked, every single time.

That story worked when I went into major credit card debt twice, paid it off completely, and kept moving forward. It worked when funding from a major grant was delayed by five months, and I had to move in with friends for a short period.

Through all these twists and turns, I realized where my source of financial support resided. As someone who grew up in a single-parent family in Alaska, barely sustained by child support and alimony (begrudgingly provided by court mandate), I had every reason not to trust the universe to have my back. Yet when I did and took subsequent action, everything that truly mattered to me - every need that ever surfaced - was met by saying "yes" to my calling. While my decisions had rocked my financial stability, I found that my stability grew in other ways: confidence in my purpose and a growing professional reputation. A new kind of wealth emerged.

Human Connection

When I began storytelling in schools and keynoting at conferences, I traveled to urban cities across the country and also flew in small planes to rural places in Alaska. I'd spend a week in a village school, sleeping on a piece of foam in a kindergarten classroom so that I could share my love of literature with children and coach them to become storytellers themselves. Each step I took created a meaningful human connection through the power of story.

When I woke up from a dream in 1984 telling me to go to the former Soviet Union, I took a leap of faith and made the trip, meeting schoolchildren who said to me, "Please come back to the Soviet Union, bring more stories and bring children to help tell them!" As a result of that request, I made eight more trips to the country. I developed the US/USSR Young Storytellers for Peace cultural exchange program which was the subject of an award-winning PBS documentary. I also founded the US/USSR Teachers for Peace Program, and starred in a Soviet-produced television series telling the favorite stories of American children, which reached 50 million viewers and earned me the title of Russia's "American Fairy Godmother."

One of the most meaningful journeys of my life took me to Seattle Children's Hospital, where I founded the Storytelling Residency Program and engaged with 1,500 patients and their families. Through the stories I told and the stories they told, we shared some of the hardest and most beautiful parts of life. One of my terminally ill patients, eleven-year-old Mandy said, "The experimental tests the doctors are doing on me are going to help other kids with my form of cancer. So, please tell my story after I'm gone. I want people to know that my life counted." When the funding for the hospital project ended, I felt that no other work could ever take its place.

A Better Boeing

At that dark moment, I was invited to deliver a keynote speech for the Boeing Company's annual Good Neighbor Campaign which raised money for United Way. The audience included CEO Phil Condit and two hundred primarily male senior leaders. Their goal: $26 million. My job? Inspire them to strengthen their resolve and get it done. It was a morning filled with laughter, celebration - and tears. Three weeks later, I got that call from Boeing. "Are you the storyteller who makes grown men cry?"

They asked me to provide storytelling workshops and individual coaching to strengthen their leadership capabilities and improve teamwork. Financially, it made perfect sense, as my financial advisor was quick to remind me. However, after working with critically and terminally ill children, the choice felt crushing.

Fifteen years earlier, in 1981 when I sat down to meditate in my backyard, I would never have seen this as part of my vision. I'd given up my path towards financial security fifteen years before to amass a different kind of richness: one that came from those human connections in the classrooms of the US and Russia, or in Seattle hospital rooms I would never, ever forget. I was facing a choice that I feared would take me away from what I loved most, transforming a child's life. Still, something called to me. Once more, I said yes.

At first, it was almost as hard as I'd feared. I had to find my footing as I worked with thousands of engineers and IT specialists who were dismissive of anything unrelated to facts and data. It was up to me to build the bridge and to make the power of storytelling relevant to them as leaders. And I did. I also found, much to my surprise, that this new world gradually revealed satisfaction as deep and powerful as any I have ever known.

Flying Free

There was the manager who had never publicly told the story of his fear of flying and how he overcame it, yet he did so in one of my workshops. That breakthrough enabled him to tell it to his own employees, only to discover that three people who worked for him had the very same fear but were too ashamed to speak of it in the workplace. His transparency freed them to get the help they needed.

My *Story by Design* training and coaching became a cornerstone in leadership programs in both the US and India, where workgroups shared stories about overcoming adversity, dealing with prejudice, facing opposition, fighting addiction and the courage it takes to live an authentic life. I served as a consultant to the Boeing Company for 24 years, transforming the workplace by creating safe and sacred containers for life-changing stories to be told, giving voice to the voiceless and deepening the regard among colleagues.

This work allowed me to buy a home, save for the future, travel and generously donate both my time and financial resources to the causes I believe in, especially in my new adopted home of Costa Rica, where I serve on the board of a U.S.-based nonprofit that raises funds for a variety of organizations across Costa Rica.

Soul Mission

To my delight and surprise, working with adults became my new passion, one that continues to flourish to this very day as I coach leaders and entrepreneurs around the world. They learn to tell their stories for the purpose of communicating the "why" behind their business, to build trust, strengthen their teams, promote their services, and inspire those around them. My work with adults is the way I pursue what my soul has always wanted: to make a difference in the lives of others and do good in the world.

Now, as I embrace my next chapter, continuing to do what I love, I've realized that sometimes the most beautiful parts of a vision are those we can't see at the start.

Real wealth comes from following your heart. Always. Do not be afraid of the dark forces along the path: those are your moments of initiation. They'll give you the chance to strengthen your resolve, and recommit to your calling. Remember to give yourself the gift of pivoting into uncharted waters that might feel foreign to your original vision. You may discover that your soul has a much larger vision in mind for you.

You will count yourself rich in purpose, knowing that because you said yes, you have inspired and enriched the lives of others. That is your ultimate source of contribution and wealth.

-Michale Gabriel

Michale Gabriel, the Founder and CEO of *Story by Design*, is an award-winning storyteller, author, coach and leadership consultant.

Starting in the 1980s, Michale's international work in Russia and Ukraine promoted intercultural understanding and gained media acclaim. Her Young Storytellers for Peace US/ USSR exchange program was the subject of an award-winning PBS documentary that aired nationally. Michale starred in a Soviet-produced film series, telling favorite stories of American and Russian children that reached 50 million Soviet viewers, earning her the nickname of Russia's "American Fairy Godmother."

Her corporate clients include The Boeing Company in the US and India, where her *Story by Design* training is the cornerstone of several gold standard leadership programs.

A resident of Costa Rica, Michale coaches private clients online, facilitates workshops, and speaks at conferences on the power of story to change lives and create an impact.

18

MANIFESTING WEALTH

BY ANIA HALAMA

"By being receptive, we can avail ourselves of the spiritual wealth available to us. By being open, we can receive things beyond what we ourselves might imagine."

- MING-DAO DENG

I grew up fairly poor, with a learned attitude from my family's perspective stemmed from the old saying that "money doesn't grow on trees". It's acceptable to say that I grew up having deep limiting beliefs around money and believing that I'd probably continue living poorly for the rest of my life. I remember thinking to myself, "If my parents are poor, how could I be wealthy?" I had to work on that feeling, sit with it and unlearn it. Eventually, I realized that I am worthy because worthiness is a birthright.

I started to notice my family's income deficiencies when I was very young, around second or third grade, usually in moments when we couldn't afford discounted lunches, nor spend a little extra on brand name foods, and resorting to the cheapest possible options. We were immigrants from Poland and had come to America when I was 3. My parents didn't speak a word of English, which landed them a few odd jobs – some even having them clean offices and houses just to pick up some extra work due to their language barriers. My parents did the very best they could. There came a day when a lot had to change, when my dad faced an unfortunate injury from his job as a welder, leaving him handicapped in one arm and unable to work. I remember translating legal and medical documents, at the age of 10 because I was the only one learning English from school. I had to step up and be an adult to help my parents.

By the age of 16, I had a full-time job. I had taken a graphic design class in high school and unearthed a passion for it. It landed me a corporate job after earning my bachelor's degree at 19. By the age of 20, I was making six figures and my dad began stealing money from me. It took a long time until I was able to forgive him.

Stress Sick

By 25, I grew physically and mentally sick from the high stress of my job and everything going on at home. I was dealing with anxiety, insomnia, and dense, dark energies. I soon stepped away from graphic design because I was so jaded and didn't enjoy designing for corporate America. I wasn't allowed to be creative, or make beautiful art – everything had to be masculine and structured when art is flowing and feminine.

I decided to quit everything and travel the world. I had to get as far away as I could from my hometown Chicago.

I started in Southeast Asia and ended up in Europe. Living abroad was cheaper, and I had more money to spend on meditation, yoga, and personal development classes. I started to self-heal through eastern medicine and reiki healing, which inspired me to become certified in reiki as well. I experimented a lot with plant medicines, which transformed the way that I deal with my physical body today. I can't remember the last time I went to a doctor, because if anything is ever wrong, I turn to homeopathic methods. Though it took some time, I was able to heal my insomnia, anxiety, and stress levels. I was also able to understand myself because I wasn't granted that time due to growing up fast and taking on adult responsibilities so early on. I was on a path to a deeper connection with my spiritual body.

He Manifested

Before I began my spiritual journey, I was dating a man who was constantly manifesting money left and right. I was amazed, so naturally, I convinced him to teach me his ways. He was well over 20 years into his spiritual journey already, and I was just starting. Coming from a corporate background, my interest in earning more money was already present from the hustling masculine energy I was tapping into all the time. I didn't exactly know how to harness the feminine nor was I aware of the spiritual aspect of attracting wealth from feminine energy. I didn't know that money is energy, and like most people, I thought that money was objectively something we work for. When I saw the way he was attracting money and great opportunities into his life, I started meditating, working closely with him, and learning more about the Law of Attraction. I was able to reprogram a lot of my thinking and leaned into attracting my desires rather than chasing them. I was then introduced to EFT Tapping.

EFT Tapping is accessible to all. It's about the focus on the meridian points in our bodies, just like in acupuncture, however, instead of pinching ourselves with needles, we tap those points with our fingers. We do cycles of mantras and start with negative affirmations and end with positive affirmations. You'd start with the side of the hand, then between your eyebrows, side of the eye, under the eyes, under the nose, chin, collar bone, and so on. There's no right or wrong way to conduct EFT Tapping; so long as you are hitting the points and starting with the negative affirmations and ending with positive ones, you'll be able to see a shift in your energy right away. I watched my boyfriend do the EFT Tapping on himself and at first, I thought it was cuckoo, which didn't work positively in my favor. Due to that initial skepticism, I wasn't seeing results and learned that our intentions and trust have a lot to do with any practice because we are required to be open to the possibilities.

Limiting Beliefs

Today, I am certified in several practices including EFT tapping, Ho'oponopono, Akashic Records, Reiki Healing, and more. I believe that we should teach from experience, and because of my experience growing up, I frequently help my clients with limiting beliefs that I once had as well. The most common limiting beliefs I see in entrepreneurs that come to me for help are worthiness issues, feeling unworthy of money, abundance, or more clients. I'm also a law of attraction coach, so I don't teach people how to work hard to get the money, I lean towards helping them merge their masculine and feminine energies to attract money and ideal clients. One of my favorite things is teaching people how to depend on their energies to attract their desires, rather than constantly hustling. In a way, I help entrepreneurs by incorporating some healthy spiritual practices into their lives.

I know how to hone in and do well with seeing tangible results from my Law of Attraction methods - like the time I manifested $100,000 in just 40 days. I help clients fulfill their manifestation goals, and it's been a fantastic journey to watch them grow from their limitations and attract their rightful successes. Alongside the choice of an eight-week or twelve-week one-on-one program with me, I offer several different group programs and courses that can be done at your own pace.

Five Years

I believe your ideal client is the person that you were five years ago. Today with coaching, I do most of my work with spiritual entrepreneurs and marketers. I started off working with people who were trying to reach $10,000 - $20,000 a month, and I've shifted to helping entrepreneurs who are already established and working toward $50,000 - $100,000 every month.

With my business, Rebel Entrepreneur, growing at the rate it has so far, I have decided to focus on the spiritual and enlightened side of my coaching and working with everyday people to connect with their souls and find their purpose. The idea of hosting my own Awaken Your Soul retreats came to me and reenergized my passion for my work, gathering people for plant medicine ceremonies, nature hikes, and various relative spiritual practices.

Goddesses, Retreat!

This boost of passion also gave me the idea to host the Goddess Forward Retreat. The event featured 15 speakers, five speakers a day, who all delved further into the many ways women can connect to their goddess energy and harness their abilities in all things, supporting growth and transformation. I've found myself gravitating toward the healing work of helping my community align with their spiritual selves to bring their wildest ideas into their physical realities.

Today, it feels so good to be based in Medellin, Colombia. I was traveling for the last six years up until the COVID-19 pandemic when I came back to my life in Medellin. I was surrounded by my wonderful friends and fellow spiritual entrepreneurs; together we exchanged many healing sessions to pass the time during quarantine while continuing with our manifestations. In fact, I've taken note of my manifestations and the funny ways that they effortlessly fall into my lap. More recently, my two friends and I decided to partner up and create a brand of NFTs, in our efforts to save the toads and jungles of Colombia.

With our NFT project, we want to give back to the land by conserving the amphibians and land while doing our part in helping the infrastructures of our jungles. As soon as we set our intentions with this project, the opportunities to expand on our idea came forth. One of my partners and I went to NFT week in Miami where we met with 300 investors, who were very thrilled about our mission. It was all in such perfect alignment, inspiring us to continue going bigger.

Medicinal Connections

My team and I are very drawn to the realm of psychedelics and plan to bring more information and healing practices around plant medicine. We are in the works of opening healing and research centers between the U.S. and Colombia. We've created great connections with doctors, researchers, and high-end investors for our plans to bring forth more healing to all humans. It's been amazing to see the logistics follow so seamlessly after identifying an idea.

I accredit most great things that have come my way to focusing on wealth on a spiritual level. It's lovely to look internally and unearth the wealth within; finding that all opportunities and possibilities can effortlessly come to us when we are tapping into the flowing energy and the state in which we can attract all things perfectly and abundantly, in divine timing.

I guess I can say that it's easy to continue building on the success of my business, writing five soon-to-be-published books, launching an environmental activism project, and surrounding myself with a community of loving people, when I'm nourishing my internal wealth.

-Ania Halama

Ania Halama is best known for her heart-centered practices in her business. Her passion is to use her eye for design, knowledge, and love for self-discovery and healing.

She has done everything from taking the big leap of quitting a corporate job to getting certified as a Reiki Master, Ho'oponopono Master, Angel Card Intuitive, Law of Attraction Master, and EFT Certified Coach. When she isn't traveling the world, helping thousands of entrepreneurs get realigned, she is a spiritual life and business mentor.

19

ABUNDANCE OF INTUITION

BY MICHELLE BELTRAN

"The only real valuable thing is intuition."

- ALBERT EINSTEIN

We all know that wealth is the measurement of what our combined assets are worth. It is the physical possessions of what we own and what can be converted into a form used for transactions. It is something we can hold, bargain with, and count. Wealth is usually a combination of things we can physically hold. However, there is a secret source of wealth we can't hold—a wealth we already own and utilize as though it was a physical asset. It is often the one stable thing that influences how, when, and where we will acquire physical wealth.

It is our intuition—our subconscious mind. The power inherent in our subconscious mind is something we should include in our list of valuable possessions. You see, it is quite possible that the powers generated by our subconscious are more valuable than the physical things we own.

Intuition—a bridge between our conscious and subconscious minds—exists alongside our sensations, thoughts, and emotions. Balancing these faculties enables us to maximize our potential and make decisions that will contribute to our overall good. Carl Jung once said, "I regard intuition as a basic psychological function that mediates perception in an unconscious way and enables us to divine the possibilities of a situation…"

Intuition is a form of knowledge that materializes in our consciousness without deliberation. It works without our knowing it. It is just there when the situation calls for it. It is not magical. It is a faculty generated by the unconscious mind that delivers hunches and prods us to act and/or re-evaluate. Our intuition rapidly sifts through our past experiences and accumulated knowledge to give us a heightened assessment of any situation or decision we may have to make.

Subconscious Protection

Intuition is the wealthy component of our spirit that protects and advises us when there is no other mechanism for deciding. It is our gift for being human. Like everything in life, you must acknowledge intuition and use it, or it will become too faint to hear. The more you listen to your intuition, and the more you act on what it suggests, the more heightened your awareness will become. Your intuition is the strongest connection you will have to your subconscious mind.

I learned how to link these two mental functions when I realized it gave me unprecedented access to the source of all creativity, wisdom, and understanding. It is the link to a new and extraordinary kind of thinking, and I wanted a piece of that.

Gut Sensing

Did you ever plan to do something and then stop because of a "gut feeling;" a premonition, a sense something is about to happen. That's your intuition. It is often called, a sixth sense, instinct, percipient, a hunch, second-sight, or just a feeling.

One of the most famous intuitive episodes was experienced by President Abraham Lincoln. He told of a dream he had filled with the sounds of mourners. Lincoln followed the weeping and crying to the White House where he found guards stationed near a casket. Lincoln asked a guard who had died. The reply was, "The President. He was killed by an assassin." The account appeared in the writings of Lincoln's close friend and biographer, Ward H. Lamon, before Lincoln was fatally shot in Ford's theater.

General Ulysses S. Grant didn't go with the Lincolns to the theater that fateful night because Grant's wife, Julie, had an uneasy feeling and demanded to be taken home. Grant, too, was a target, but escaped unscathed because of his wife's premonition.

I didn't realize at first that my intuition was such a useful resource. But, when I learned to tune into it, it guided me in discerning the honesty and trustworthiness of a person or situation. It is intuition that makes us look twice at something or someone sensing when something is off.

We call that "hinky," which is another way of saying that your intuition is working.

We must learn to be quiet and let that intuitive self-speak to us. It does have our best self-interest at heart. If we can get out of our own way, put away the self-doubt and just listen, we will be amazed at what we can learn.

It is quite possible that intuition is hard-wired into us as a species. Intuition is closely aligned with self-preservation regarding every instance we encounter. Surely our ancestors wouldn't have survived very long if they didn't listen to those feelings and urges that told them when a food source was near, or when they were about to be pounced on by a saber-toothed tiger.

Ponder This

Take a moment now to consider your past few days. Have messages of knowing or hunches or hinky feelings emerged? Let that memory come in. Don't look for it. Don't search for it. Let it find you. Did you have a feeling that someone you had not seen for some time would call and then receive a call from them? Did you find yourself saying, "I knew it," after an event? Was there an inner knowing about a decision you had to make? Did the perfect words or artistic inspiration come to you at just the right moment with a feeling of exuberance or excitement?

Perhaps, out of what seemed like nowhere, you had an inspired idea that resolved a particular issue of importance. That's you, listening to your inner knowing. That's the start. That's your intuition guiding you.

Inner Wealth

We seldom realize that all financial wealth has a ripple effect affecting who we are on a broader level. Our financial success in life is rooted in our thoughts, beliefs, and perspectives about money. It colors the choices we make, how we think about things, the perspectives we hold, and the belief systems passed on to us that we allow or don't allow in.

Through our own self-actualization, spiritual and emotional clarity, and awareness, we can have a life of abundance that we seek on all levels, not just financial. The only obstacle comes when we reject what is the spiritual, emotional, and psychological parts of ourselves.

Money has a life force all its own. We establish a relationship with it. Everyone holds a different view of money. It means different things to us at various points in our lives or experiences. Our thoughts about money change by what surrounds it at a moment in time.

Warren Buffet was asked to describe the difference between getting rich and being wealthy. He responded, "People seeking riches never have enough. Wealth is a state of mind. Wealthy people always have enough."

Are you in a wealthy state of mind? The state of mind begins by holding a sense of abundance within your thinking and being. A deep-seated feeling of abundance extends far beyond the stock market. It is something embedded within us.

It is not an emotion to put on or a burst of energy that comes to us. It is the peace of knowing that what we possess is enough.

My Wealth Steps

It is an understanding of true wealth that allows us to usher in financial wealth. When we are shaken to our core, we are motivated to change. On the heels of a very challenging time, I launched my business. Year one found the business producing a six-figure income—a tall order for one woman. I believe this happened because I found true wealth first. I was not seeking financial wealth. In fact, only when I found true wealth, did financial wealth find me. Here are the steps I took to create financial freedom and it's not quite what you might be thinking:

Face It

Get real with yourself and face the truth of your life. That means being honest about what is real in your life at this moment and using that information to guide the choices you make. Do an honest financial and spiritual assessment of your life today. Do an honest evaluation of your beliefs about money, the people who surround you, and the people who are important to you today. Identify where you are and where you should be and embrace it or change it.

I believe life is not meant for amassing oodles of stuff or sacrificing meaningful relationships or life experiences to gain security or fame. At the end of the day, you have you—and that's enough. Ask yourself: Would you regret not making a lot of money? Or would you regret not spending time with the people you love deeply? Are you at peace with yourself? Is there a material or tangible item to which you are tethered that prevents you from participating in meaningful experiences? Could you do without that item? I asked these questions of myself and found massive awareness in the answers. There was much attention to things that meant nothing and no attention to those things I really valued.

Surrender Mindset

It's human nature and somewhat innate to want control. It feels safe. I encourage you to surrender. Control is a myth. We never really have control. There is always something bigger than us—the bank really owns the house; job security only exists at the behest of an employer, and a life tomorrow is not promised to us. Once you begin to embrace the surrender mindset an interesting thing happens, you feel freedom. You begin to see the benefits of surrendering your fears, ego, perfect plans, and the illusion of control. I certainly did. I found that the moment I dropped my attempts to control everything, plan for every possible scenario, and to dwell on past transgressions, my life leaped forward in an instant.

If the pursuit of a goal sacrifices the most important things in your life, it may not be worth it. There is an old saying, "Is the juice worth the squeeze?" Excessive or unrealistic sacrifices, in the long run, don't work. Be mindful of the sacrifices you're making and at what cost they are coming.

When True Wealth Arrives

True wealth arrives when you have made the conscious choice to live life on your own terms. Living life on your own terms is what complete freedom is all about. Learn to balance your heart and your mind to manifest the life you deserve. Financial freedom and wealth are meaningless without this.

Remember it's not the financial wealth you're after. In fact, it's not even the concept of money that pushes you to want money. What you, and all of us, are really after is the freedom to do as we please, when we please. Money is merely the vehicle to bring us to that state of financial freedom.

True wealth and real financial freedom are having the latitude, and the choice to enjoy the time that brings the most joy into your life. Marie Kondo, the organization guru, has her clients ask if everything in their closets brings them joy. If it does not, it gets donated or discarded. She is on a mission for others to find out what sparks joy in their lives—even if it's just a spatula. She illustrates the fact that joy is important even in the small things you own. She works to have each client find complete joy in their home and in the things they own.

To be wealthy in life is to know joy. It is also to appreciate all aspects of what it means to be human—to be present in the moment for those you love and for those who need your love. It's to be self-aware, to live with purpose, and to be committed not only to one's own happiness but to the happiness of others.

Looking back at my childhood, I believe that growing up in an accepting environment where spiritual concerns were commonplace made it easy to explore the important role my subconscious and my intuition played in my life. I learned early that the spiritual part of us does not exist by accident. The unspoken urge which prompts us to be wary or to explore an idea is not accidental. The foundation for being wealthy beyond our expectations is laid by who we are, inside and out.

Is wealth having a private jet, a dream home, or an expensive car? Of course not. We know better than to measure wealth by those standards. We know those things don't necessarily bring us wealth. Things are merely an indicator of monetary wealth—a wealth that may or may not be satisfying.

So today, reach for the dreams you didn't think were possible and begin manifesting and creating your life—the life you were meant to live; a life that makes you and those around you feel alive and fulfilled. Look for the joy in all you do.

-Michelle Beltran

Michelle Beltran is a best-selling author, globally celebrated intuitive expert, transformation trailblazer, and spiritual teacher.

She has become a leading international authority in the spirituality arena, specializing in psychic functioning, mediumship, and remote viewing.

She is the host of a popular psychic development podcast, The Intuitive Hour: Awaken Your Inner Voice.

Having appeared at numerous spirituality and wellness summits and magazines, including *USA Today, Forbes*, and *Hay House World Summit*, she has worked with thousands of people across the globe. Michelle's greatest joy is seeing people engage in more fulfilling lives and teaching them how to awaken, amplify and trust their inner voice.

This former probation officer has traveled throughout the Far East living among men, women, and children who rarely had enough to eat and who struggled for personal self-advancement. This life-changing experience deepened her commitment to assisting others in transforming their lives.

Her competitive spirit and passion for healthy living led Michelle to many years as a professional cyclist and lifelong fitness enthusiast. She finds that much of the clairvoyant information she receives in her work is related to nutrition, health, and fitness and she credits competitive sport with the gift of medical intuitiveness she now shares with clients.

Currently based in Northern California, when Michelle is not deeply immersed in authoring her next engaging read, you'll find her West Coast Swing dancing to the current jams of the day or cruising on her Orbea summiting the next biggest climb she can find.

20

ANCESTRAL WEALTH

BY GENEVIEVE SEARLE

"A woman armed with ancestral wisdom is a powerful force."

- LORI BERGMAN

My grandmother's life was full of broken dreams, grief, loss, and virtual exile from her community. In her final three years, she was denied access to her five children, and died of pancreatic cancer, heartbroken and alone just months after her 36th birthday. I arrived 12 years later, on the exact day that my grandmother would have turned 48. This synchronicity is not lost on me.

I feel a deep soul connection with the woman whose eyes I never saw, whose birthday I share, and whose stories I carry in my bones. One day I hope to tell her full tale and honor her legacy of a WILD woman born too early for the world.

Forging Abundance

My mother, despite the loss of her mother and her

own early trauma, forged a life of abundance. She raised three children and only recently retired from her successful psychology practice. My father has always been a great support to her as she found her way, though I don't think my mother has ever truly *thrived*.

My mother and grandmother's stories of grief, loss, trauma, abuse, and abysmal self-worth were then passed on to me, not intentionally but genetically.

Before I emerged into the world these stories of despair had been *epigenetically imprinted* onto half of my DNA.

My Mother's Trauma

As an egg inside the ovaries of my infant mother, while she was still in my grandmother's womb, I vicariously experienced both of their lives; their environment, the food they ate, their relationships, and yes, their traumas, were all experienced by me in some way. Even without that direct connection, our bodies have a brilliant way of passing on information to future generations through the process of epigenetics.

Epigenetics is the science of how we interact with the world around us. This is a dynamic, ongoing, and real-time relationship where we are assessing and responding to our environment, preparing for what's to come. Everything from food, light, temperature, habits, relationships, and thoughts, influence epigenetics. This is what I call cracking the ancestral wealth code. It's about reading and rewriting our spiritual and physical DNA.

Genes, DNA, and Imprinting

Epigenetics works above the gene, by not altering the genes but altering their expression. Much like a light switch, that turns a light on or off but doesn't change the actual wiring.

Epigenetic *imprints* happen when we experience something so big that we are forever changed and/or we experience or choose the same thing repeatedly. Our bodies pay attention to things it deems important and stores this information for future use and reference.

If deemed important enough, imprints can cross over into subsequent generations, even when there is no contact with the original person or direct memory of their experience. I feel this is the case with me and my grandmother.

Our Bodies Tell Our Stories

The Cherry Blossom Mouse Study reveals the brilliance of epigenetics. In this experiment, male mice were repeatedly traumatized by an electric shock that they associated with the scent of cherry blossom. Two generations later after artificial insemination, meaning that the original male mice never had direct contact with the female mice, their offspring not only went into a trauma response when they smelt cherry blossom but were also born with neurons in their nose to detect the scent early on. This enables future generations a better chance at avoiding potential danger.

Like the mice, our bodies tell the stories of our lives and the lives that came before us. We are walking anthology books that stretch back to the dawn of humanity.

Encoded into my system was my grandmother's story - the one that says that if I am too big, bold, or different, I will lose my children, be outcasted from my community, and die alone.

This fear ran through me at a deep subconscious level for many years, leaving me with immediate and long-term physical symptoms whenever I stepped up too boldly or uniquely. As a child, I always felt torn between shining my fullest expression and dimming my light, lest I was to lose everything.

We are Not Powerless

As I grew up, I dealt with scoliosis. It minimized my full energetic force, kept me "small", and created a host of downstream effects, like poor circulation and gut issues. I believe this was a subconscious response to ancestral imprints as well as my experience of sexual abuse and rape.

However, I am not powerless, and neither are you. Within the pain and grief, there are also the gifts of insight, wisdom, and love that could not come any other way.

Every person and experience that came before us brought us into this body, at this time. We are born with roots, both "good" and "bad", and without them, we wouldn't exist. Every experience, including the awful ones, brings its own gift. Additionally, we are not from one single lineage but like the threads of a tapestry, we are woven together from many lives, stories, and experiences.

With this awareness, intention, and commitment we not only alchemize the trauma of generations into something beautiful and powerful but also use the traits in our ancestry to shape our lives and THRIVE!

Little Love Notes

The treasures that live within us are astonishing! They are woven into us, wrapped in our DNA like presents, or tagged onto them like little love notes. The riches of our inheritance are often not recognized, nor easily quantified, but available if we know how to recognize them and learn to tap into them. Looking back on our sprawling family trees, our potential powers already exist and are thus woven within us.

I believe that we desire to become our ultimate versions because it is sparked into recognition by those around us who shine it back to us.

Living Elixirs of Potential

No one carries the exact same blend of inner resources and potential - not even identical twins. While our DNA might be the same, experience and environment sculpt us differently through the process of epigenetics.

Our true potential lies in the combining of our internal forces. Like living elixirs, we are a unique blend of our ancestry, experience, and environment. As we enhance certain attributes through focus and aligned action, we alter the molecular structure of this elixir and ourselves.

When leaning into different parts of our ancestry we bring different traits and gifts to the forefront. We are conditioned to look outside of ourselves for our fulfillment, convinced of our lack, thus missing what sits within us ready to be awakened.

Your Inner Alchemy

With this knowledge, we can change negative patterns, limiting beliefs, and even physical traits, by alchemizing them into something beautiful and powerful.

Asking questions like, "Who lives in my family tree?", "How can I see this differently?", and "Who already has the imprint for who I wish to become?" is a powerful way to begin this process.

The Keys in Your DNA

Maybe it's a grandparent, aunt, or someone further back, but it's almost guaranteed that someone in your line has gone first in the area that you want to enhance. We may not like them as a person, or how they live their life but there is still magic in knowing they carry a key to our evolution. We come from millions of people dating back to the dawn of humanity, and through this we carry built-in archetypes in our very bones.

The Value of Our Traits

My parents brought me up on a diet of philosophy, psychology, moderation, and a deep connection to the Earth - all of which allow me to see the systemic nature of life and feel radical compassion. I see patterns and links in a way that many people miss. I greatly value the traits they've passed down, but there are others that I can call forth to live my fullest potential and actualize my soul's desires - the courage to be daring and bold, with a wild vision for the evolution of an abundant, financial savvy humanity.

Wealth is Knowing What You Are Made Of

Looking into my family tree I found my aunt Narelle; a daring, fun, playful, and successful entrepreneur who created a life of true abundance. Her DNA also runs within me, and I am able to lean into this knowing that her strengths are imprinted into me, waiting to be amplified.

Combining the emotional intelligence, wisdom, mental awareness, and ethics gifted to me by my parents with the vision, creative daring, and financial savviness of my aunt, alongside the fortitude of a thousand generations in my bones, I know I carry a potent blend of possibilities through epigenetics.

In my life and my work, I fuse the combination of functional breathing, ancestral awareness, body connection practices, and transformational mentoring with the most game-changing cutting-edge health and wellness software available.

PH360 Epigenetic HealthType profiling software is based on over 11 branches of science and can read the body through hard data like body measurements. It determines which hormones have been most dominant during growth and development, and how they influence everything from physical appearance to mental predispositions.

Discover Your Genetic Genius

This software uncovers natural genius, helps streamline the body, and significantly enhances mental and emotional wellbeing. Covering six key areas of life: nutrition, movement, social, environment, lifestyle & career, it offers insight into who you are, how you operate, and how to craft your life to maximize your innate brilliance.

With this next-level wellness technology, fused with emotional intelligence, ancestral awareness, functional breathing, and spirituality grounded in practicality, I offer something beyond life-changing. This is wealth.

As a Wellness Reclamation mentor, my mission is to support humanity in the reclamation of holistic wellness, self-love, and personal power. When people operate from this place, they shine, and the world rises with them.

I call myself The Optimisation Queen, which is my company name, as an invitation for people to also claim for themselves. I'm not here to be a guru for people to cling to forever - I'm here as an advocate for personal sovereignty and the global shift.

Radical Responsibility

We have been convinced that our health and wellness are too complicated for us to navigate ourselves. We hand our power over to others, eroding our sense of self and dimming our potential. The truth is, we have everything we need already encoded within us. We are far more powerful than we have been led to believe.

These are the questions we ask when we are ready to THRIVE and live our fullest truth, deeply connected to the call of our souls. This is true WILD wealth and it's available to YOU!

- *Who am I?*

- *How do I work?*

- *How does my unique physical being need to eat, move, breathe, connect, rest, work and live to be in flow?*

- *What stories live in me from my own life and from those who came before me? How can I turn these into my greatest assets?*

- *How can I know and love myself fully and deeply so I can connect with others in an open-hearted, generous, and mutually powerful way?*

- *How can I craft my life to optimise my genius so I can radiate my unique brand of brilliance out into the world?*

- *How can I be my Ultimate Self and how can I support others to do the same?*

You are the distilled essence of all who came before you. A potent elixir crafted from more than a thousand generations and your ancestral stories waiting to be told in a whole new way, blended with your unique experiences and gifts. You ARE the medicine and the true wealth waiting to be revealed!

-Genevieve Searle

Genevieve Searle is best known for being the Optimisation Queen and has spoken on the TEDx Talk stage with How to Thrive in an Era of Uncertainty.

She is the #1 best-selling author of *Embrace Your Feminessence: A Must Read for Every Woman Who Wants to Embrace Their Power, Women Gone WILD Wealth Edition*, and *Illuminate Your Feminessence*.

She is also a ph360 Endorsed Health Coach, Buteyko Breathing Instructor, Thor Laser Practitioner, Flowstate & Ecstatic Breathwork Facilitator, Transformation Catalyst, Ancestral Nutrition Mentor, Colon Hydrotherapist and veteran of Women's Wisdom work.

Working with Genevieve comes with the warning label "Enter at your own risk, you will not be the same woman after working with me."

When she isn't speaking on massive stages, she can be found dancing, writing erotic poetry, being a great mother to her 3 sons, and ally to her lover of over 20 years.

21

BECOME AN ASSET

BY DANELLE DELGADO

"When you learn, teach. When you get, give."

- MAYA ANGELOU

You need to become an asset yourself in order to truly become wealthy. When your talents, abilities, and wisdom are the value to offer the world your wealth can never be taken away. I thought it was money that I was seeking, but the blessings of single parenting, cancer, business building through world shutdowns, pandemics, and beyond have given me the gift of knowing that wealth is who you become, and when you become it, your bank accounts in money, relationships, opportunities, faith, health and all areas of life will be multiplied.

It's priceless, to know that everything will work out because you have the resourcefulness to handle it.

When you realize that you are the asset, you will gain what I call *Unstealable Everything* – Joy, Success,

Money, Confidence, Competence, Freedom, Fun, and Opportunity.

You may have met many people of influence, wealth, or recognizable stature and noticed a similar strength, generosity, fierceness, and that *something extra* that most others just don't naturally have. It's not simply charisma, it's even beyond character. Those pieces are necessary, yes, but it's not just that. It's that personality that seems borderline arrogant, but not quite. It's a vibe of confidence that emulates fearlessness and calm in any storm. They are always the biggest giver in the room, yet quietest until their time to speak, a legend that fills a room with hope, truth, and excellence in the shortest amount of time. It's those who have built a life so competently, that it is clear and congruent. They need not ever impress another, but their impact on others is imminent.

Build Yourself

So, how do you become an asset? Do the work to build yourself into one. You can build whatever you like if you are willing to do the inner work that builds outer wealth. What you build, will be responsible for building you! Building what no one can take from you is the key to building real wealth.

THE 6 STEPS TO BECOMING AN ASSET

Step One - Go the distance to win, repeatedly, until you learn what it takes.

Learn that winning is always possible if you are willing

to work for it and finish what you start. I mean it, what if you were all you had, could you conquer anything? Would you? Or would you quit? There is a knowing that comes from doing the work to build oneself to a point that it doesn't take the help of others to win - but others are always welcome there to accelerate the journey. The outlook to achieve in this step is that losses are lessons, trials are teaching moments, and winning is a lifestyle.

Step Two - Be okay with the scary human that comes out in the middle of all that fear, pain, and trouble along the way.

This bubbles up as you tame your inner beasts and build habits that build a champion, not a practicer. I had a mentor who once told me "If you want to see who someone really is, bump them and see what spills out… watch them in a challenge, if you like what you see, that's a champion, if you don't, that one you avoid."

He was right: The moment I decided there could be more to life, I was being bumped everywhere in my life, and what spilled out was *UUGGGLLLYYYY.*

I will share how learning this step played out for me: My first round of wealth was built *in lack*, total dire need, and fear. I had three jobs, was newly divorced, and alone, not knowing how I would feed, clothe and shelter my family of 2-year-old twins and another child 16 months older. I was in complete shutdown mode, praying for a miracle, hoping that sales and learning this new language and way of life were my ticket out.

If I could just work more hours than others, I could outsell them. "Sell to everyone," they said, "if they don't buy, are they really your friend?" With my bulldozer approach to try and save my own life, I was bumping and breaking everyone that I knew. I didn't care what others thought, I was just going to prove everyone wrong, that I was a winner, that I was not worthless.

I was being bumped and what spilled out was pain, fear, self-loathing, insensitivity, carelessness, and promises I couldn't deliver. I did it all wrong! And hey, I wouldn't have loved me back then, either.

So, be okay with all of that, forgive yourself, and then use it to your advantage. What I learned here in Step Two, is you will be embarrassed in public on the way up, which accelerates the growth process! No one wants to be humiliated, especially in public, so I was on a mission to clean up my act. I knew I had to quit acting from pain, which deteriorated business and detracted people from me. I had to become a human that was skilled, not sloppy, organized not accidental, trusted not doubted. I had to become the one my results required.

Step Three - A commitment to learning as a lifestyle.

People have asked, "How'd you do it so fast Danelle?" Well, the pain of losing was excruciating, so I learned faster than my competition. I read, studied, and earned until I could afford the best mentorship. Then, I scaled myself, as committed as I had ever committed to anything. My losses were big, and they showed me my biggest weaknesses, so I studied them, and worked on the opposites which became my antidotes! I would win an award or an honor and get the attention of a legend and pay, earn or give my way into their teaching so I could accelerate. I became a human people knew would follow through, learn fast, and make it count. I was committed to growth.

Step Four - Do it for yourself, true to yourself.

Sometimes along this path to winning you can lose sight of who you are and do what others do. I did it for the eyes watching first, then I did it within. Yes, it happened to me for sure, I believed I was as superhuman as the human they introduced at the mic, I believed the press and that I was *amaziiiinnngggg*. When in truth, I was just on my way and had so much to learn. Many humbling experiences happened in this season. It was a critical part of my rise to discover who I really was, as a winner and loser, and how I wanted to live this life.

I began to live a life congruent to my own beliefs, values, and compass and not anyone else's. I tapped into my mission, vision, and values, and I began to only do things that agreed with all of that. I learned how mentorship can guide, but it can be damaging if not done in a way that you become more tapped into yourself. I became a stronger version of myself, principled to do life on my own terms and around only my rules.

Step Five - Learn to build because of others not for yourself.

Once you know how to win, that is not the celebration time, it's when you have learned something so powerful it can serve, help or even save another. I started looking at the faces of those I would help. I knew that the better I got, the more impact I could make for them.

I started asking others who doubted themselves, "Have I helped you?" This is a total shift. Imagine if I had quit in the middle? Ask yourself today, "Who will lose if you don't win?" This was a breakthrough! There was no longer pain in progress, instead, it was energetic magic. When I could win, I focused on others. Talk about a rocket ship! We must each grow to a point that we know our best is not just possible but *required* in life. My true wealth was found in those I could impact because I was willing to grow into a human who could make such an impact.

This journey to wealth is building yourself into the greatest human asset you know, the human heart people love to be around, the mind they want to weigh in on ideas, the collaborative who trusts themselves enough to show up for others, the one who is cool and concentrated on solutions, not problems –this is an asset. You become someone who increases the odds of winning for others, because of what you have done for yourself, so people want you as a part of their life and business.

Step Six – Self Control is critical.

Yes, there will be forces of evil on your road to good. Understand this, you develop a special kind of self-control in learning to win even while being cheated, mistreated, beat down, and embarrassed along the way. You become the human in control enough to be brought into the world's biggest challenges, for you can be counted on to finish with class. This piece is critical to becoming the one everyone can trust when something can only be done by a seasoned professional. When you realize you no longer have the option to lose it, quit or fight back, then it will always be a winning season. You must know that every relationship counts, and every response and move matters. When you can control that, you can control your path.

A winner is one who has won and lost a lot, who has built, rebuilt, lost, and then rebuilt all again to ensure they could do it every time – better, faster, and stronger. That human has been to the races and back a few times. That human that has been up against the strongest of battles and challenges and comes through innovating and conquering with a smile. That human that has been cheated, hated, mistreated and you watch them rise in complete self-control. No matter what the world throws their way, they simply seem ready, trained, and equipped for anything. That person, that winner, is who you would choose to rise with.

That is wealth. Becoming an asset.

The lessons I learned on this path allowed me to define who and what I needed to be. It took me many years to learn the true art of wealth building – that every step of the journey is about becoming the one your results require. So, I had to get clear on my goals and what my desired results were. I have been building myself into a human who is ready for anything. A trained, equipped, connected, resourceful asset that people love to build their life and do business with. This kind of human is the one who gets invited to the biggest opportunities in the world. This person becomes one of the most valuable players because of the time invested to prepare for game day.

This journey to wealth made me an asset, and that has built me wealth that could never compare to just income. I am one of the most connected humans in the world, one of the most respected women among men and women in business, one of the highest-ranked speakers and innovators for global brands, one of the biggest strategists to help people earn, and one of the humans most committed to teaching others how to win big and **give back like crazy**.

The person you must become on this journey can only be earned. It cannot be gifted or taught. Go become an asset and then true wealth, the *unstealable kind*, will be yours.

-Danelle Delgado

Arising from the fires of life, the now serial entrepreneur Danelle Delgado began her journey when faced with raising her three small children on her own. Forced to make a change she went from struggling to survive, to award-winning success in business by persisting her way *in*; she aligned with world-renowned business experts and gained them as her personal mentors. Danelle built multiple high-producing income streams and become a skilled sales professional and elite mentor to numerous high-performance entrepreneurs. Over the past 7 years she has built multiple companies, done millions in sales, and even landed an appearance on NBC's

The Apprentice in 2012 as a top sales earner and guest judge on the show. In 2015 she launched her 4th company, a live training event platform called *Life Intended*, that has brought leaders such as Darren Hardy, publisher of *Success Magazine*, Grant Cardone, 5X *New York Times* Best-Selling Author, Todd Stottlemyre, 3X World Series Champion, and more to Colorado to speak alongside her. Expanding globally with a *Life Intended* live platform in Australia as well as with her multiple online training academies and elite retreats for high-earning entrepreneurs from St. Maarten to Italy, and beyond. Danelle is one of the most highly regarded training experts in the industry and quickly became the go-to female to train sales and business strategy worldwide.

Melisa ♡
Wishing you so much joy +
abundance as you create
beauty in the world!
♡ Robin

22

THE WELL OF SOURCE IS THE SOURCE OF WEALTH

BY ROBIN MULLIN

"To become as the well, the ever-replenished well which holds all things, is to become the one you truly are."

- THE GUIDES THROUGH PAUL SELIG

Aladdin had his genie; Cinderella had her Fairy Godmother; Luke Skywalker had The Force. Throughout history, in all cultures, myths and stories relate how invisible helpers make wishes come true for those with sincere hearts.

We each have our own version of a magic wand or creative force to support us. It is called many things including God, the Universe, Divine Intelligence, the Great Mystery, or the Wild Unknown. My name for this infinite pool of possibilities is the Well of Source. It is the point of origin for wealth and well-being.

This mysterious power is often thought of as separate from us and difficult to access without a minister, shaman, or spiritual guide. Separation is an illusion, I've learned, that connecting to Source is a choice, like dipping your cup into a well. With sincere intention, commitment, and clumsy practice my relationship with Source has become intimate. Maintaining more consistent connection has helped me magnetize homes, jobs, relationships, creative ideas, and amazing experiences beyond my wildest dreams! In sharing my journey, I want to support more wild women in manifesting wealth of all kinds with increased speed, ease, and joy.

The Gift of Mystical Experiences

Sometimes the soul gets shifted by experiences and places one could never predict. At several pivotal points in my life, unexpected and unexplainable events seized my attention and demanded I consider a new perspective.

Such "mystical experiences" are portals to encounters beyond understanding. Each of the dozen times they have occurred, I was in an unfamiliar place with a sincere inquiry in my heart. At the age of twenty-four, unemployed, in an abusive relationship, and feeling lost, I spent my savings on a spontaneous trip to Egypt and Israel. Sitting near the Saqqara pyramid, playing with a milky quartz stone I found in the sand there, I was transported to an ancient temple. I watched myself enter different rooms to observe healing practices using sound to tune organs of the body. A week later, at the Church of the Beatitudes near the Sea of Galilee, I felt a deep connection with Mother Mary that had my heart pounding. Experiencing collective suffering, I sobbed for an hour with tears of compassion. Years later, at another transitional point in my life, I was transported into the weightlessness of the cosmos, floating among the stars while bathing in a sacred Spring in Bali. I am deeply grateful for each of these transformational gifts; they recharged my soul's connection to Source and gave me courage and insight to make difficult life-changing decisions.

Early Glimpses into Eternity

These unexplainable experiences seemed familiar and comforting to me. This is likely because my earliest years allowed a prolonged period during which the veil was thin between this world and the unseen one. Born with sight labeled "legally blind," I saw only color, light, and energy, but no defined shapes. My parents were known to me by smell, sound, and feel, and I navigated by the perception of different energy vibrations, including sensitivity to emotions. I lived in my beautiful, blurry world until, at two and a half, I got my first pair of eyeglasses – baby blue, cat-eye style with thick lenses. Sitting on the lawn for hours, I was amazed to discover individual blades of grass and tiny bugs.

How relieved I was though each night when I could take off my glasses and return to my familiar world of light shows and dancing colors. Blurred lines and connection were what I knew; I loved to hug and touch all things. Feeling and intuiting my way forward as a child served me well in navigating various states of consciousness as an adult.

I Got the Chills

Consciously connecting with supportive Source energy helps magnetize outcomes in tangible forms. So many desired results have manifested with invisible help, and what fun it is to see how my requests show up, often more spectacular than I imagined. Amazing homes, with resources coming from unexpected places, have delighted me! Once visiting Hawaii, I got chills when I saw a house that had shown itself to me in a recent dream. We had no intention of buying a house in a rural old plantation town, but my intuition told me otherwise. A sudden and surprising financial gift showed up to make the purchase possible. During the next eight years, soul-shifting experiences and connections were nearly constant.

Circumstances suddenly changed when we needed to return to California and find a larger home with room for my mother-in-law. It was not a favorable time to sell and my new home wish list put buying way beyond our budget. Someone suggested a home exchange, and I wrote to six California homeowners about the possibility of a trade. Within two days, one responded whose house was a perfect size in my ideal location, and we happily traded houses for four years.

My Definition of Wealth

Wealth, to me, is not a large bank account or accumulation of physical items, but the ability to create whatever is needed in true alignment with my soul's best life. Well-being on all levels – Physical, Mental, Emotional, and Spiritual – is the best expression of wealth.

The speed and ease of attracting holistic abundance have increased as I focused on building a sincere relationship with the Divine Mystery that I call the Well of Source. I tend to it like a sacred marriage in which I made a vow to honor and respect the unseen forces as they care for me. I love knowing the same stardust that is the essence of all things swirls in my blood and bones. When I am experiencing life most abundantly, I am aligned with my soul and something infinitely larger.

Keeping the Channel Clear

Maintaining a pipeline free of mental and emotional debris requires us to routinely remove obstructions to our flow. We each will find ways that work best for us to do this. My personal clearing practices include silence, meditation, journaling, sunset walks, creating art, and time in nature. Others practice dance, music, or a sport. Anything that calms and centers is a valid clearing tool.

A clear channel helps us give and receive easily, allowing universal love to flow through us and into the world. As we radiate harmony, joy, happiness, health, beauty, healing, and compassion, we generate movement of energy toward ourselves, others, and desired outcomes.

Keep Blessings Circulating

Though our culture gives us fear-based messages to hold and accumulate wealth, doing so can block the flow of love and joy coming our way. Imagine holding every breath a little too long! Clinging to what we receive is counter-productive to living with a healthy and energized body, mind, and spirit. Granting blessings is as important as opening to receive them; it keeps Source energy circulating. When we are filled with gratitude and joy, there is a natural desire to share. Spreading blessings every day feels wonderful and keeps our energy flowing.

Consciousness Is Conversation

Universally, spiritual masters teach that mindfulness or conscious awareness is key to individual happiness and collective harmony. Evolving consciousness requires excellent communication. Begin with careful listening as the foundation of a good friendship, a strong marriage, and a fulfilling parenting experience. Listening- with attention, keen interest, and curiosity - is also critical to a blissful relationship with God or Source.

The world around us is always in conversation, inviting us to listen and join in. Cultivating ways to hear whispers of guidance gives access to all kinds of information and support. Because tuning in to guidance has proved so important for me, I chose to teach my children about it early on. Close to their tenth birthday, I introduced the concept of listening to God, intuition, and nature spirits and took each child on a first "vision quest" trip.

Vision Quest For My Children

I carefully chose a different location, an unfamiliar and wild place of quiet and beauty, for each quest to fit my son's or daughter's interests. Embracing the concept of a special weekend adventure with mom, each enjoyed a unique experience. One son found it difficult to relax and listen in a meadow on Mt. Shasta but had a creative flow of ideas when hiking and climbing rocks. My other son easily sat for three hours of solo time near Boynton

Canyon in Sedona, Arizona. He wrote in his journal and surprised me with a story of the message a hawk told him. Vision quest trips for my children continued through their teen years. All three are exceptional listeners with keen intuition who have manifested abundance on many levels, including scholarships, wonderful relationships, and their dream careers.

Dreams are also an important source of guidance. I began working with dreams in my early twenties, following my first workshop with Dr. Brugh Joy, author of *Joy's Way*. Dreamwork has been a powerful tool that I trust to guide me. Learning how our subconscious cleverly uses the language of symbols and images, offers insight into current situations, and can give us a glimpse of the future. Dreams can provide emotional healing, signal danger, and help provide answers to problems. Receiving a transformational dream affirms an internal shift. The *Talmud* says, "An unexamined dream is like an unopened letter."

The Power of Community

Participating in the fellowship of a committed spiritual community is greatly valued across cultures and has contributed enormously to my development. I love asking life's big questions within sacred circles. Intimate study groups provided me with safe settings to explore creativity, spirituality, feminine mysteries, expressive arts, and skills such as Voice Dialogue. Close friendships are formed as members share authentically. Witnessing the magic emerge from the collective wisdom in circles always delights and inspires me. Effective circle groups and communities may stay together over decades, like The Inside Edge Foundation, where I served as Board President for four years. Co-founded by Diana Wentworth in 1985, the power of this community has nurtured emerging spiritual thought leaders like Jack Canfield, Barbara Marx Hubbard, Mark Victor Hansen, John Gray, Barbara de Angeles, and many others. My forty-year involvement in sacred circles with my treasured mentor, Carolyn Conger, has provided a vehicle for steady personal and spiritual development. It fueled my passion to create *Wisdom Circles*, my passion project offering safe, intimate, and expansive experiences for others.

Trusting Invisible Help

It is up to each of us to refine our personal relationship with the Well of Source. Our listening expands as we pay attention, keep the channel clear, and invite new ways to receive messages from invisible help. Trust what comes and stay faithful to your Soul and Source. Holding tight to any particular result is never helpful. Make requests and let them go, trusting in a great outcome. As Carolyn Conger says, "You don't need to force anything; what is yours will come to you. Just say 'thank you' for everything that comes."

Do You Feel the Call?

In response to the challenges and needs of our time, many of us are feeling called to mobilize our talents. It is up to us, my wild women sisters, to bestow our wisdom and blessings to be in service in unique new ways. In the words of author and spiritual teacher Jan Phillips, "We are the ones we have been waiting for."

I invite you to amplify your abundance through conscious partnership with Source. Walking your own path, you will delight in discovering unique ways to experience wealth and well-being as you give and receive. Living a life in sacred relationship with the Well of Source is as magical as having a genie lamp or texting a message to your Fairy Godmother!

-Robin Mullin

Robin is a visionary leader, community builder, and passionate advocate for personal and collective evolution. Her MA in Organizational Leadership was granted from Chapman University, where she also became an adjunct professor. In her corporate and consulting roles, she helped build cultures where innovation and creativity thrived. Robin has served as Executive Director of several nonprofit organizations and President of *The Inside Edge Foundation for Education*. Robin is the Founder of *Wisdom Circles, LLC*, which offers a variety of intimate group experiences supporting conscious evolution, wisdom, and creativity. Offerings include online and in-person groups, retreats, and circle leader trainings.

For information, private consultations, and resources, visit the *Wisdom Circles* website. Robin is a grateful mother of two sons and one daughter. She is the enthusiastic grandmother of three. She lives in San Clemente, California with her husband, Harry, and their faithful dog, Alopeke.

WE ARE WOMEN GONE *WILD*
WE ARE *Courageous.* *WILD*
WE *Celebrate* OTHER WOMEN'S SUCCESS AND
Cultivate THEIR DEVINE FEMININE GIFTS.
WE ARE ALIGNED WITH OUR SOUL'S *Purpose.*
WE LEAD WITH OUR *Heart* AND LIVE BY
Example FOR THE NEXT GENERATION.
WE KNOW VULNERABILITY IS *Strength*
WE RESPECT *Prosperity* AND TRACK THE MONEY LINE.
WE RECEIVE WITH *Gratitude* AND ACT WITH GRACE.
WE USE OUR *Gifts* FOR GREATER GOOD.
WE *Support* OTHERS LESS FORTUNATE.
WE ARE *Kind* WITH OUR WORDS AND STRONG WITH OUR STAND.
WE EMBRACE *Wealth* AND TRUST OUR *Intuition.*
WE DEVELOP *Leadership* AND WELCOME *Diversity.*
COME BE *WILD* WITH US!

Get All Your Bonuses Here

www.WGWBook.com/Wealth-Edition-Authors-Free-Gifts/

ACCESS TO AUTHORS

ADRIANA MONIQUE ALVAREZ

Email Address: adriana@adrianamoniquealvarez.com

Website: AdrianaMoniqueAlvarez.com

ANIA HALAMA

Email Address: contact@aniahalama.com

Website: AniaHalama.com

APRIL RYAN

Email Address: rediguana8@gmail.com

Website: Red-Iguana.com

BARBIE LAYTON

Email Address: intuitivebarbie1@gmail.com

Website: YouAreAmazingTV.com

BLAIR KAPLAN VENABLES

Email Address: blair@blairkaplan.ca

Website: BlairKaplan.ca

CAMBERLY GILMARTIN

Email Address: camberly.gilmartin@gmail.com

Website: WGWBook.com/Camberly-Gilmartin/

DANA KAY

Email Address: dana@adhdthriveinstitute.com

Website: ADHDThriveInstitute.com

DANELLE DELGADO

Email Address: danelle@danelledelgado.com

Website: DanelleDelgado.com

DIANA WENTWORTH

Email Address: dwvww@aol.com

Website: DianaWentworth.com

EBONY SWANK

Email Address: ebony@shopswankaposh.com

Website: ShopSwankAposh.com

GENEVIEVE SEARLE

Email Address: hello@theoptimisationqueen.com

Website: TheOptimisationQueen.com

HANALEI SWAN

Email Address: hanalei@hanaleiswan.com

Website: HanaleiSwan.com

ISABEL FAGAN

Email Address: Isabel@TopTalentJV.com

Website: www.TopTalentMag.com

KAREN WHELAN

Email Address: whelank787@gmail.com

Website: SoulutionTherapist.com

KORTNEY MURRAY

Email Address: wild@coastalkapital.com

Website: CoastalKapital.com

MICHALE GABRIEL

Email Address: michale@michalegabriel.com

Website: MichaleGabriel.com

MICHELLE BELTRAN

Email Address: mbeltran@michellebeltran.com

Website: MichelleBeltran.com

RHONDA SWAN

Email Address: support@rhondaswan.com

Website: RhondaSwan.com

ROBIN MULLIN

Email Address: robinmullin918@gmail.com

Website: Wisdom-Circles.com

SHAR MOORE

Email Address: shar@sharmoore.com.au

Website: SharMoore.com.au

STEFANIE BRUNS

Email Address: info@businessflowacademy.com

Website: BusinessFlowAcademy.com/en

TARRYN REEVES

Email Address: tarryn@tarrynreeves.com

Website: TarrynReeves.com